monsoonbooks

A SERVANT OF SARAWAK

Dato' Dr Sir Peter Mooney was admitted to the Faculty of Advocates in Edinburgh and was called to the Scottish Bar. He was then appointed Crown Counsel, Sarawak and rose to become acting Attorney General and Public Prosecutor in Sarawak as well as a member of Sarawak's Supreme Council (the cabinet) and Council Negri (the legislature).

Dato' Mooney left Sarawak and the service of the Crown for Kuala Lumpur in the early 1960s. Here he became founding partner of leading Malaysian law firm Skrine and, over more than four decades, has earned an exceptional reputation at the Malaysian Bar. Dato' Mooney served as the Vice-President of the Malaysian Bar, Chairman of the Legal Profession Committee of the Malaysian Bar and Chairman of the Complaints Committee of the Malaysian Bar.

In addition to his legal practice, Dato' Mooney has been the chairman, director or governor of many hospitals, schools and charitable organizations in Malaysia, and was appointed Honorary Consul of Ireland in Malaysia.

Dato' Mooney was conferred the honour of Knight Commander of the Order of St. Gregory the Great by His Holiness Pope John Paul II and the rank of Dato' Bergelar (Dato' DiRaja) by HRH the Sultan of Selangor with the personal title of Dato' Kurnia Bakti DiRaja.

A SERVANT OF SARAWAK

REMINISCENCES OF A CROWN COUNSEL IN 1950S BORNEO

PETER MOONEY

monsoon

monsoonbooks

Published in 2015
by Monsoon Books Pte Ltd
www.monsoonbooks.com.sg

Editorial / Sales:
No.1 Duke of Windsor Suite, Burrough Court,
Burrough on the Hill, Leics. LE14 2QS, UK

Registered office:
150 Orchard Road #07-02, Singapore 238841

First published in 2011.

ISBN (paperback): 978-981-4358-37-8
ISBN (epub): 978-981-4358-38-5

Copyright©Peter Mooney, 2011
The moral right of the author has been asserted.

All rights reserved. No part of this publication may be reproduced,
stored in a retrieval system, or transmitted, in any form or by any
means without the prior written permission of the publisher, nor
be otherwise circulated in any form of binding or cover other than
that in which it is published and without a similar condition being
imposed on the subsequent purchaser.

Cover and inside-page photographs©Peter Mooney

Printed in USA
17 16 15   1 2 3 4 5

CONTENTS

Foreword

Dato' Dr Sir Peter Mooney and I are both legal practitioners. However, it was not through the practice of our profession but because of our involvement in the medical profession that we got to know each other well. This was when Dato' Mooney was the Chairman of the Assunta Hospital, a charitable hospital founded by the Franciscan Missionaries of Mary, and I was invited to be his Deputy.

Dato' Mooney has spent much of his time offering his assistance to various Malaysian charitable causes and has also carved out an impeccable career and earned a tremendous reputation at the Malaysian Bar.

It thus gives me great pleasure to pen this foreword for his memoir.

I find his memoir, a draft of which was extended for my reading, extremely interesting, readable and difficult to put down. It certainly serves to entertain and educate.

However, and more importantly, this memoir serves as a historical record of the culture and customary practices of the indigenous people of Sarawak. As the region has progressed and developed, the colourful and unique practices of its people have inevitably been compromised and sadly may, in time, even disappear. This memoir preserves their history and will be a source of research to historians and anthropologists.

From a legal perspective, this memoir records the judicial and legal practices existing in Sarawak during the relevant period, while giving us an insight into the way Dato' Mooney carried out his practice of the law. Again, without such a record as this memoir, matters of interest and import will be forgotten as time goes by.

I recommend this memoir unreservedly and hope that Dato' Mooney will now find the time to write about his years in West Malaysia.

Tun Zaki Tun Azmi
Chief Justice, Malaysia

Foreword

In 1961, I began my pupillage in the now defunct firm of Bannon & Bailey, then the largest and one of the most established law firms in Kuala Lumpur. The late, and much respected, John Skrine, was supposed to be my pupil master, but he went on long leave to Ireland, and that was when Peter Mooney became my de facto pupil master. He was a most exemplary pupil master in all respects, a privilege that very few, if any, new lawyers would be able to get today.

I was told that he was a former Attorney General, but at that time (and until I read this memoir), I had not realised what a distinguished career he had had, short as it was, as the chief law officer of the colony of Sarawak.

My admiration for Peter as a man, and not only as a lawyer with a heart, has gone up many more notches after reading his accounts of his early life—how he was brought up and educated in school and college, as a rising advocate in Glasgow, Scotland, as Crown Counsel and Attorney General of Sarawak, but especially as a young soldier who fought with the British Fourteenth Army (under the command of General Sir William Slim in the Burma Campaign against the Japanese

Fifth Army under General Mutaguchi). He fought so that we might have our today.

His terse and subdued account of his involvement in one of the most famous and bitterly fought Second World War campaigns in Asia, and his observations on the Japanese soldiers, show a very human and humane side of Peter that many might not have known.

Peter's humanity shines forth from his accounts of his easy interactions with the people of Sarawak, especially the indigenous peoples. His linguistic flair enabled him to learn and speak Malay and Iban very quickly. His affinity for the way of life of the various races living in Sarawak, their customs and culture, and his compassion and understanding of their condition are evident from the colourful vignettes of his experiences whenever he had to travel to the interior of a vast territory with no roads in order to lay charges and prosecute offenders.

Lawyers and judges who are friends or acquaintances of Peter will find it absorbing to read about his experiences as an expatriate who did not lord it over the natives in a world and time now past. My only regret after reading it is that the book is too short and that there must be much that is left unsaid.

The legal community of Malaysia has gained something intangible from Peter's decision to move from Sarawak to Kuala Lumpur to spend the rest of his professional and natural life. I look forward to reading the next part of his memoir of his life in peninsular Malaysia.

Chan Sek Keong
Chief Justice, Singapore

Preface

When I arrived in Sarawak in 1953 the country was as it had been for centuries. There had been little development. There were no major roads. The small towns were situated on the great rivers that divided the country and travel between towns was by Chinese commercial launches, which sailed downriver and out onto the South China Sea then along the coast and up the appropriate river to the desired destination. There was no radio or television. There were few telephones and these communicated within their towns. Such newspapers as there were, were in their infancy and had very limited circulation. The majority of the population lived simple lives in the interior as subsistence farmers and had virtually no communication outside their immediate neighbourhood. Contact with the world outside Sarawak was by a weekly ship from Singapore to the capital, Kuching.

The age of cheap intercontinental flights and mass tourism had not dawned. Only the occasional wandering journalist came. He saw no beggars, no malnutrition, no smoking factories, no drug addiction and no crime, and wrote lyrical articles on the last paradise or wrote of headhunting, which had formerly been common. The evils of capitalism had not yet descended on Sarawak, nor had many of its benefits.

This was the country in which I arrived. It was happy and peaceful. I thought that I had come to civilize the people. It was they who civilized me. They were friendly, warm and most hospitable, ever willing to share what little they had. Moral standards were high. It was hardly necessary to close windows or doors at night. Theft was almost unknown. This memoir relates of major criminal trials but it must be kept in mind that these occurred over a period of seven years. Crime was not, as it is today in many countries, a social problem. There was no army and none was required. The police force was small and had no need to be larger.

This was a period that could not last and I consider myself fortunate to have experienced a small part of it.

Peter Mooney

Childhood and a Question of Identity

I was born in 1923 in Donegal, a remote and very beautiful county in the extreme north-west of Ireland, bordered by the Atlantic Ocean to the north and west and by the British province of Northern Ireland to the east.

At the Catholic primary school to which I was sent I was given a sound basic education. I was studiously inclined and came out top of every class. At the age of 12 I finished my primary schooling with the school prize for General Excellence and was fortunate to be accepted by a college belonging to the Society of Jesus. The teachers were Jesuit priests equipped with university degrees and the Jesuit character of long religious training. They entered me for a competitive scholarship, which I was awarded and it paid my fees. My studies, apart from general studies, religious knowledge and some science, were English, French, Latin, Greek and Mathematics.

The Jesuits were learned and warm, with a sense of humour and they knew how to handle boys of all kinds. They gave me an excellent all-round education for which I am ever grateful. It gave me a secure foundation for life. They entered me for the ancient University of Glasgow, founded in AD 1451 by a papal bull of the scholarly Pope Nicholas V, founder of the Vatican Library in 1448. I passed the entrance examinations and was awarded a scholarship, which paid my fees. I entered the Faculty of Arts, which was situated in the old buildings of the university comprising two quadrangles separated by wide, dim cloisters and containing two major halls: the Bute Hall, built with funds gifted by a former Marquess of Bute, and the Randolph Hall. Very grand staircases led up to these halls, which were used for various functions, including that of examinations. I chose Humanity (the term for Roman studies comprising Latin language and literature and Roman history and civilization), English Language and Literature, and History as my first year subjects.

When I entered the University of Glasgow, I was just 17 years of age. Conscription had been introduced in Britain and every able-bodied man of 18 and above, with certain necessary exceptions, was required to enter the British Armed Forces. Refugees from countries invaded by Germany, many of them members of the armed forces of those countries but also many civilian refugees, arrived in Britain. Britain became an armed camp full of soldiers, sailors and airmen.

I was Irish and not liable for conscription as Ireland was neutral during WWII. However, all my university friends went off to the armed forces and I felt that I should be one of them. I went to the army recruiting office and was interviewed by the recruiting officer. He told me that since I was a volunteer I could choose my regiment. I chose the Royal Scots, which was the oldest infantry regiment and had a distinguished history. It was the only regiment entitled to wear the royal tartan known as Royal Stewart. Its headquarters were in Edinburgh, a short distance from Glasgow. Before I left his office, the officer told me that he would like to give me a piece of advice. 'You will become an officer,' he said, 'so just remember this. Before you order a soldier to do anything, you do it first. Then he will respect you and follow you. If you want him to jump over this table, you jump first.' This seemed to me to be excellent advice and I tried to follow it throughout my military career.

During this period at the university, there was heavy bombing by the German Luftwaffe on Glasgow. The city is situated on the River Clyde, which opens out into a magnificent estuary with a considerable volume of shipping from all parts of the world. The city itself had large dock areas, major shipbuilding yards and numerous factories. Inevitably it attracted the attention of German bombers.

As part of my duties as a cadet in the university officer training corps, which I had volunteered for, I had to spend many nights perched precariously on top of the University Tower and on the apex of the high-pitched Gothic roofs of the old buildings of the university armed with a bucket of water and a stirrup pump to deal with any phosphorus fire bombs that might land on the roofs. Fortunately none did since I gravely doubt that my ability to negotiate in the dark the precipitous hazards of the steep roofs to get at any flaming bomb, particularly with the modest equipment given to me, would have enabled me to extinguish any fires. I had, however, a spectacular view of the city since the university is situated on a hill overlooking much of it. After darkness fell there would be heard a wail of sirens giving warning of the approach of enemy squadrons of aircraft and soon we could hear the droning of their engines in the sky above us. The air became filled with hideous sounds: the crack of the anti-aircraft guns surrounding the city, the crashing sounds of the high-explosive bombs detonating and the destruction of buildings. Flames from burning buildings caused by fire bombs added to the horror of the scene. Most of the city's population sought refuge in air-raid shelters, which had been hastily constructed. Searchlights probed the sky and anti-aircraft guns continually fired at the bombers, albeit with little success. Peace arrived when morning broke and the bombers had departed. I would descend from the lurid scene and the horrific din, still in uniform, to a calm and learned lecture on Virgil in the Humanity class underneath me in the very building on which I had spent the night. In the Humanity lecture room I was in civilized surroundings and immersed in the literature of a great civilization. It was a marked contrast to the barbarity of the scenes of the night. Many innocent people had just died, or were dying, many were seriously injured and mutilated, and many had lost their homes and all they had. To put this out of mind was not easy.

It was during this period that there came to my notice, without warning, something of which I never had any inkling and which had a major effect on my life from then on. I had been brought up in a family of four sisters and two brothers. The father had died when I was a young child and I scarcely remembered him. The mother was the head of the family. I had always been treated as her child and a member of the family and had no reason to think otherwise. I was too young to realize that the age of the lady whom I regarded as my mother was such that I was unlikely to be her son and to reflect on the discrepancy between my age and the age of those I regarded and was brought up to regard as my siblings. One evening I received an invitation to meet a certain gentleman in unfamiliar surroundings. I had no idea why I had been invited but I went and met him. We were alone. I learned then that the purpose of the invitation was for him to tell me that I was his son. I was stunned by this news. The shock was such that I was unable to think. I said nothing at all and the meeting ended. I spent the night in thought. How had all this happened? Many questions came to mind and I had no answer to any of them. Why had nothing been said about my being brought up by a foster family? My identity was not what I had been led to think it was. Even the name by which I knew myself and had always been known by others was not my name. Why had I not been told of this before? Why was I being told about it now and with much left untold? My mind was in a whirl.

I said nothing of this to anyone. For as long as I had been aware, I was with the foster family, all of whom knew that I was not a member of the family. They had, for reasons unknown to me, said nothing to me and called me by a name that included their family name and which could not be mine. After this meeting, when I was with them I said nothing about the meeting. I and they behaved as before. I was grateful to them for receiving me as a member of their family and never in any manner treating me as an outsider. However, a gulf had arisen between my life spent with them and my university and social life. I kept them in separate compartments. Whether the family knew that I was now aware that I was not one of them I did not know but I could no longer introduce them to anyone as family. Nor could I introduce anyone whom I knew to the father who had suddenly appeared in my life. I had no filial feeling for him. Filial feeling cannot be created overnight and there were too many unanswered questions which I did not feel that I could raise since the information had been withheld from me. I did not think of him as a father. I was invited to dine with him and his wife from time to time. His wife was not my mother. They had no children. Whether she knew my history I do not know but she showed no interest in me, and my relationship with her and my father was merely polite and with the respect due from the young to elders. I never spent a night under their roof. This man informed me that I would be his heir. I had no interest in the inheritance and experienced no disappointment when it never came to me.

War and My First Taste of the East

My studies helped to distract me from my identity crisis but it was not long before I attained the age of 18 and my life was changed again by a summons to leave the university and enter the army. I entered as an officer cadet and was sent to an officer cadet training unit in Kent in England. The rigorous and arduous training in the unit was designed to make us into soldiers and fit us for being commissioned as officers. It left little time for thinking of personal affairs. Army life and discipline was very different from anything that I had been accustomed to. Living was rough, the training was physically and mentally challenging and the discipline strict. We had intensive physical training, assault courses, weapons to learn to handle, drill and parades, lectures and battle training. Our time was more than fully occupied from reveille, the sound of the bugle calling us from sleep, until late in the evening when we were thankful to get to bed.

However, the commandant of the officer training unit decided that I and other university cadets needed more basic training. We were sent to the recruit training wing of Maidstone

Barracks in Kent and had six weeks of being knocked into more soldierly shape by regular non-commissioned officers of the Royal West Kent Regiment. It was a salutary experience and went far in transforming us into the soldiers we were supposed to be and building a new dimension to our personality.

It was also a new experience in that I was amongst recruits from all parts of Britain and very different in background, upbringing and culture to my own. Their accents were unfamiliar and some of them almost unintelligible. Accent and mode of speech were a mark of social class in those days when there was no TV and radio was relatively new. Regional and class accents had not been modified by these new impacts on social life. There had to be mutual adjustment. People like me were of a different social and educational background from the majority, a difference that was obvious in many ways to the young soldiers we were with twenty-four hours a day, sharing the same challenges and tests of character. As officer cadets we were not in a position to mix with the new recruits on equal terms. We had to learn to adjust to them and they had to learn to accept us and free themselves of any misconceptions. We were learning much about life and maturing rapidly in the process. Subsequent service in the army was spent initially on exercises and in training in various parts of England and Northern Ireland. During my training in Northern Ireland I had no opportunity to cross the border into the neutral Republic, although Donegal, on its north-western tip, is adjacent to the British province of Northern Ireland. Our military exercises were held throughout Northern Ireland but my brigade was based in Antrim and subsequently in County Down, in the beautiful Mountains of Mourne. Indeed all of Northern Ireland was beautiful. In all of this we were being prepared for active service in one of the theatres of war.

In the army we lived in barracks or in camps. We were apart from the civilian community and had little or no relationship with them. However we were aware of the caste division between the Protestant and Catholic communities, which was very obvious. The Protestants were the ruling majority in the British province. They had mostly been brought from Scotland by Oliver Cromwell in the seventeenth century whereas the Catholics were native Irish, dispossessed of their lands and still regarded as an inferior class. There was thus a difference of race and temperament and culture as well as of religion. Newspapers of the day contained advertisements of employment that invariably contained a statement that no Catholic need apply. It also became apparent to us that the police were entirely Protestant. Doctors and other professionals always seemed to be Protestant and those in authority of any kind that we encountered were Protestant. The oppression by the Protestant majority, which had ruled the Province since the partition of Ireland by the British Government in the 1920s, led to the violence that began in the 1960s. However, within the army we were unaffected by this and there was no religious prejudice amongst officers or men; the only difference amongst us was the necessary one of rank.

After some months of training in Ireland the time came when I was sent back to England and equipped for going overseas into a war zone. We sailed from the great port of Liverpool, after marching early in the morning from the railway station through the streets to the quay. Young women hurrying to their work, seeing our youth and knowing that we were bound for overseas and the war, rushed into our ranks and embraced and kissed us, pressing into our hands cigarettes and gifts of any little thing they had. We were much touched by their spontaneous kindness, generosity and concern for us.

We embarked on a great ship, formerly a passenger liner but now crammed with troops, and sailed down the Mersey, looking back at the great Liver Building, Liverpool's prominent landmark. Once in the Irish Sea we then sailed north and arrived in the wide Clyde estuary, where we joined a convoy of ships. We sailed in convoy, escorted by destroyers protecting us from submarine attack, and our course took us south through the Irish Sea and then west into the Atlantic. We were never told where we were bound for but we knew from the sun and the stars that we were sailing south. We had sight of a coastline on our port side, which could only be Spain, and easily recognizable was the narrow Strait of Gibraltar as we entered the Mediterranean Sea. We passed safely through the Mediterranean and then entered the Suez Canal, which we transited without stopping.

At night we sailed in total darkness, with daily emergency stations and constant watch for enemy submarines. It was a long voyage. Pacing the deserted, darkened decks when on duty at night, one could see a myriad of stars overhead and our wake was spangled with phosphorescence sparkling like diamonds. All was silent except for the quiet throb of our engines and the soft swish of the sea, parted by our bows and passing glittering along our sides. By this time it was evident we were going to India, probably destined for action in the Fourteenth Army, which was in combat against the Japanese Army in Burma.

Our first stop was Bombay. There we disembarked and encountered a novel host of sights, sounds and smells. This was my first sight of the East. Little did I think that I was to spend most of my life in this environment. Before we disembarked we were issued with Wolseley helmets, so-called after a Field Marshal who lived a hundred years before our time. They were large, white, with a metal spike on top, a wide visor, and a low, sweeping backpiece to protect the neck. Along with this imposing headpiece, and quite incongruous with it, was a mosquito net consisting of a small cap with the net hanging all around to cover the face. It was dark green, like the jungle uniforms we were subsequently issued with, and difficult to see through. We were also issued with dark green mosquito gloves. All these items were completely useless and unsuited to jungle warfare or indeed any kind of warfare. They were very soon discarded.

We spent some time in tents in a transit camp at Kalyan outside Bombay with little to do. I occupied my spare time learning Urdu. My principal memory of Kalyan is of the raptors. The troops' mess tent, where meals were consumed, was located about fifty feet from the cookhouse tent where the soldiers collected their meals in mess tins, one held in each hand. The kites circled high above the gap between the tents. As soldiers crossed from the cookhouse tent to the mess tent, kites would dive with astonishing speed, pick up food from a mess tin, gauging the distance to a millimeter and never disturbing the tin, then soar aloft. Troops fresh from Britain were unused to this bold aerial piracy and were easy marks until they learned to bend closely over their tins while they crossed the gap. Even then the keen-eyed, watchful and clever kites found victims.

Travelling east by train across the subcontinent, we found ourselves in Nagpur train station on a stifling hot Christmas Day. Standing on the platform behind tables laden with food were a number of British ladies, presumably the wives of government officials stationed there. They had given up this special day and the coolness and comfort of their houses to spend the afternoon on a railway platform serving Christmas dinner to the troops. One meets goodness, consideration and unselfishness everywhere and it is always a special joy, whether these qualities are shown to others or to oneself.

We continued our journey by train until one evening we reached the wide Brahmaputra River, which had its origin far to the north in the Himalayas. We transferred to a ferry and sailed by night, reaching the other side of the river the next morning. We then advanced by vehicle and on foot. When one or two soldiers succumbed to heat exhaustion while marching, we left them with an escort to be picked up by vehicle later. We were aware that one can die very quickly from heat exhaustion unless the body temperature is speedily brought down.

After several hours of marching we reached our temporary destination near the town of Comilla in eastern Bengal, now known as Bangladesh. We were in a rough jungle camp housed in palm-leaf huts, known as bashas. It was the time of year of the chota monsoon or little monsoon. The monsoon was little in the sense of short, but the rain was far from little, it poured heavily and incessantly and we waited for a clear sky. As soon as it became a little clearer we took off in Dakota DC3s, twin-engine propeller-driven planes. The weather was still appalling but the planes belonged to an American squadron of daredevil pilots and they were undaunted. We were unable to climb over the weather and we had a very turbulent flight through thick, dark clouds, sitting on the floor of the aircraft, which was completely bare inside, and being thrown about all over it. We flew over the mountains separating us from Burma and landed at an airstrip at Indainggyi in the forest on the upper Chindwin River, a major tributary of the great Irrawaddy River, which flowed all the way south to the sea at Rangoon. We were now in the Fourteenth Army under the command of General Sir William Slim, whose book on the Burma Campaign has been compared by critics to Julius Caesar's classic memoir on the Gallic War, which I had read at school.

From then on we were in active combat against Japanese forces, which had driven British forces in Burma back to the very border with India but there had been held. It was the turning point of the Burma Campaign. The Japanese Fifteenth Army commanded by General Mutaguchi launched an attack intended to be the spearhead of the invasion of India. The

Japanese forces contained soldiers of the Indian National Army led by Subhas Chandra Bose. They believed that if they could get to the railhead at Dimapur they could sweep down into India and that India would rise against British rule. Dimapur was in Nagaland, about twenty miles from the small township of Kohima. Kohima was at the summit of a mountain pass and was considered the best route into India. The Japanese had to take Kohima in order to advance on Dimapur. General Slim decided that the Japanese forces had to be held there and an epic battle was fought at Kohima, which resulted in five thousand British and seven thousand Japanese deaths. There is now a monument at Kohima, which reads:

When you go home
Tell them of us and say
They gave their tomorrow
That you might have your today

This was a quotation from the Greek poet Simonides, writing of the battle of Thermopylae in 480 BC, where a small Greek force under Leonidas held up the vast Persian army.

The Japanese soldiers were very brave, fierce and tenacious. We admired these qualities in them but their cruelty to prisoners was not admirable. We had no hate for them, as one sees in some films of the war. They were doing their duty, as we were. They were fanatically loyal to the Emperor but they were the enemy and our duty was to oppose them.

Our task was now to drive the Japanese back and regain

control of Burma. Innumerable memories crowd in of jungles, mountains, the great forest, wide rivers, torrential rain and everything sodden, our small tents afloat in mud, blazing heat, sparse villages of Chins, Kachins or Burmans, and also of moments of great excitement, raids, the bombardment of Mandalay, the battle of Meiktila, ever-present danger, rough and uncertain living, sudden moves, shortages of water and of food, which sometimes had to be airdropped. Because we slept on the ground in very small tents we had to be wary of snakes and scorpions but our main enemies, apart from the Japanese, were mosquitoes. Malaria was rampant and we had to take Mepacrine, an anti-malarial tablet, every day. It was a harsh vivid yellow in colour, unpleasant to take and it turned our skin yellow. However, it warded off malaria or at least suppressed the symptoms. As young men, there was, as far as my experience goes, no thought of death and little fear. We took each day and incident as it came and were alert to take whatever action was necessary. There was no time for introspection.

I heard about the death of President Roosevelt of the United States and the dropping of the atom bomb on Hiroshima while I was in a tiny tent under heavy rain at Meiktila, after the crucial battle which led to the capture of Mandalay and the regaining of central Burma. The full implications of the bomb were not then clear but the moral question was unavoidable. I wondered about this without coming to any conclusion. It is sometimes very difficult to distinguish what is right from what is merely expedient. The battle opened the way to

Rangoon and the end of the campaign, which was hastened by the surrender of Japan after the second atom bomb was dropped on Nagasaki. Winston Churchill wrote: 'Never, never, never believe any war will be smooth and easy, or that anyone who embarks on the strange voyage can measure the tides and hurricanes he will encounter. The statesman who yields to war fever must realize that once the signal is given, he is no longer the master of policy but the slave of unforeseeable and uncontrollable events.' The military regime in Tokyo who launched the invasion of South East Asia were not aware of this and thousands of the youth of Japan and of the Allied forces paid with their suffering and their lives for the ignorance or indifference of these leaders.

We entered Rangoon in late 1945 and I remained there until 1947 with little to do except routine duties. At various times I had under my charge, as well as British soldiers of my own unit, Gurkha soldiers, West Africans and Japanese prisoners. The Gurkhas were our camp guards and were strict in their duties. When I returned to the camp after being out at night they would not let me in, although they recognized me, unless I gave them the correct password. I didn't understand the Japanese prisoners who were in working parties. They had a bad reputation for ruthless cruelty but they had endured the same hardships and danger as we had during the campaign and we treated the prisoners with respect for their dignity as human beings. I observed on many occasions our soldiers compassionately giving them cigarettes and other little luxuries. The Japanese soldiers were invariably most polite, respectful, obedient and hardworking. Whatever they were asked to do, they did and did very thoroughly, better than my own soldiers would have done.

After the cessation of hostilities, on a visit to Japan, I met by chance a man of my own age. We discovered that he had been a soldier in the Japanese Fifteenth Army commanded by General Mutaguchi and that we had both been in combat against each other in Burma. He embraced me as a comrade and took me to meet his family and warmly entertained me to dinner. Ordinary people do not cause wars, they are generally caused by those in power over whom the ordinary people have little control. On that visit I saw, standing outside a temple, a man in immaculate army uniform. He had lost an arm and was blind. He stood erect, unmoving, in silent and sad dignity, mutely dependent on offerings from passers-by. Years later in Kuala Lumpur, I would have a colleague who had also been in the same conflict, in the Indian National Army which was part of the Japanese Fifteenth Army. He was an idealist hoping to liberate India. India attained liberation soon enough but this might have been more unlikely had General Mutaguchi's assault on Kohima been successful. Japan's concept of a Greater East Asia Co-Prosperity Sphere was not welcomed by the inhabitants of countries it had already conquered and these territories were not administered in the interest of the inhabitants.

In 1947 the time came for my release from the army. I returned to Britain. We sailed in January from Rangoon. The last we saw of it was Shwe Dagon, the great Buddhist temple surmounted by a gilded dagoba and spire, highly visible on its hill over the city. Someone said to me: 'There is a saying that if you look back at the temple as you leave, you will return.' I paid little attention to this since I had no thought of returning but it proved to be true for me.

The Law Beckons

I was sorry to leave the East and apprehensive at the thought of being on my own, in charge of my life, out of the army and its familiar routines and orders. One gets very used to people in authority taking the big decisions and deciding our daily routines. In Britain, out of the uniform which I had worn for five years, I felt uncomfortable, uneasy and a very different person from the boy who had entered the army five years before at the age of seventeen. In the army I was surrounded by comrades with common interests and objectives. Out of it I was alone.

I was uncertain what to do now and had little sense of a direction in life. My father met me and had a proposal to make regarding my future. The proposal was of no interest to me and displayed how little he knew me. Further, I had no wish to be beholden to him since I never regarded him as a father or addressed him as such. I decided to continue my university studies and seek in them a maturity of thought which, despite five years of army service and war experience, I felt that I didn't possess. Before I left the university for the army I had studied Latin under a very distinguished Latin scholar; English literature under an equally distinguished scholar, an authority on Shakespeare; Anglo-Saxon and the origins of the English language; and I had begun history studies. After a good deal of thought as to which discipline would give me the most suitable mental training, I decided to read for Honours in History and regretfully relinquished the other subjects. However I continued to read, with interest and pleasure, the great Latin authors, English literature and some Greek. I graduated Master of Arts. In the course of my history studies I had taken a particular interest in Constitutional History which necessarily involves some acquaintance with the law, and I went on to study for a law degree. I did well in this field, collected various prizes and a scholarship. I was invited to deliver courses of lectures and the income was a welcome help.

At the beginning of my return to university I had some thought of taking the examinations for the Administrative and Foreign Service and I spoke to the Civil Service Adviser at the university. The idea of public service appealed to me. On the recommendation of the adviser, I submitted to three days of written examinations, psychological tests and assessment by a team of professionals from various disciplines to gauge my suitability. At the end of this and after considering the reports given to it by the team, the Civil Service Board expressed interest in offering me an appointment. However, by the time all this was over I had decided that I ought to complete my university studies. My performance in my law studies came to the attention of the Civil Service Adviser in the university and the result was the offer of a very handsome scholarship on the basis that I would seek admission to the Bar. The scholarship would pay the considerable fees involved and provide an allowance which would be enough to live on for my first two years at the Bar. In return for this I was to undertake to accept an appointment in the Colonial Legal Service. It was emphasized that I would not necessarily be offered any appointment and that usually they would want me to have five years experience at the Bar before making any offer. If they made an offer and I declined it, I would have to repay all that they had expended on me. This seemed very fair. I knew no one at the Bar or in the solicitor branch of the profession and could have a difficult time getting started. I had little capital to live on. I accepted.

This meant a move to Edinburgh since this is the seat of the Court of Session and the High Court of Justiciary, the equivalent of the English High Court. It is also the home of the ancient Faculty of Advocates, membership of which is the prerequisite of admission to the Scottish Bar. It was a very different world. Edinburgh is very scenic. Glasgow is much older but Edinburgh was and is the capital. Glasgow's ancient architecture was largely swept away in the nineteenth century when, surrounded by coal and iron fields it became a great industrial city. With the River Clyde and its magnificent estuary as the gateway to America, it had become a major trading port, with shipbuilding as a world famous industry. Edinburgh on the East Coast and facing the North Sea was much colder. The character of the inhabitants was different and I missed the earthy sense of humour and egalitarian manners of the people of Glasgow.

I attended Parliament House, the seat of the courts and of the Faculty of Advocates, daily, at first as a devil, the term for a law pupil, preparing opinions, drafting pleadings and writing notes on precedents to assist my devilmaster in his work and gaining experience in what would be my work upon admission to the Bar. My devilmaster, a leading junior counsel who subsequently became a judge, never advised me or commented on my work. He lacked a warm and friendly personality but he was able, was much in demand as counsel and had plenty of briefs, which kept me busy and stretched my mind.

On arriving in Edinburgh I found a small private hotel which catered for semi-permanent residents. I took a room there and made the acquaintance of the other residents, mostly students or other young people preparing to enter one of the professions. Amongst them was a girl, Avice, who was in an accountant's office and in the midst of her chartered accountancy examinations. We had common interests and rapidly became close friends, going for walks, attending concerts, university balls and other events.

As I became more involved in Parliament House, I had to leave the hotel and shared a flat in the New Town, built by the Adam brothers in Regency times, with a fellow devil whom I had known at university. Jock's only drawback was that he had absolutely no idea about cooking so when we did not eat out the task fell to me. I cannot claim to be a cordon bleu chef but Jock was not one to complain. He subsequently became a Sheriff, a Judge with very wide civil and criminal jurisdiction over one of the counties of Scotland.

Every day we walked from our flat, across Princes Street and up the Mound with the ancient and formidable castle looming above us, past the National Gallery and the Royal Scottish Academy across the High Street leading down through the mediaeval town to Holyroodhouse, the ancient royal palace, past St. Giles Kirk and into Parliament House. This was the seat of the Court of Session and the High Court of Justiciary, the superior Courts of Scotland. Also situated in it was the Advocates Library, the home of the Faculty of Advocates.

The time came for my admission. I presented my petition to the court but before I could be admitted to the Bar I had to provide evidence to the Faculty that I had had a liberal education and that I also was educated in the law. My Master of Arts degree was evidence of the former and my Bachelor of Laws degree was evidence of the latter. However there was a further requirement. I had to pass the oral entrance examination of the Faculty and the members would then ballot on my admission. The Clerk of Faculty informed me that I was to write in Latin a paper on a thesis from the Pandects of Justinian, the 4th-century Roman Emperor who codified the great mass of Roman Law. My paper would be circulated to members of the Faculty who would impugn it and I would defend it. This ordeal proved to be much less alarming than it at first sounded. The writing of the paper presented me with no difficulty in view of my university studies, which required frequent essays in Latin. The study of Roman Law including Justinian's Pandects, was an integral part of my law studies. The clerk informed me that he could provide me with a paper on the thesis from his archives if I was not up to writing one myself and that I must frame three questions in Latin—or he could supply them from his archives—and give one to each of three members of Faculty, who would put these questions to me and I would give previously prepared answers. The balloting would then take place by selected members putting either a white ball or a black ball in a bag. The black ball had thoughtfully been mislaid a long time ago and there was no risk of being blackballed. It all sounded archaic but ceremonies are an important part of life and this elaborate and solemn ceremony did impress upon the intending advocate the responsibility which he was about to undertake in the administration of justice

So, on the appointed day, dressed in white tie and tails, I followed in procession the Faculty officer with his wand of office, the treasurer, the clerk and the dean, through the library to the Octagon Room where members of Faculty, similarly dressed but with wig and gown—their customary daily dress— were standing around the walls. The dean took his seat at a small table in the centre. I was introduced and invited to read out my paper. When this was done, the dean invited any member who wished to do so to question me on it. Each of the three members to whom I had given a question put it to me and I gave my answer. Then the balloting took place and at its conclusion the dean informed me that I had been admitted to the Faculty as a member. The procession then reformed and I followed it back through the library, across Parliament Hall, where in the days before the Union with the Parliament of

England in 1707 the Scottish Parliament had had its meetings, to the Court of the Junior Lord Ordinary. Here I took an oath of allegiance to the Queen, and the judge admitted me to the Bar. I donned wig and gown, came out, shook hands all round and that was the beginning of my professional career.

Queen Elizabeth had only very recently succeeded to the throne. The proclamation of her accession was read out by the Lyon King of Arms in his picturesque garb at the Mercat Cross, just outside Parliament House and he announced that she would be known as Queen Elizabeth II. This aroused strong protests from the Scottish Nationalists. There had been a Queen Elizabeth in England and the new Queen was entitled to call herself Queen Elizabeth II of England, but there had never been a Queen Elizabeth of Scotland. King James VI of Scotland, when he succeeded to the throne of England, called himself King James VI of Scotland and King James I of England. The Scottish Nationalists insisted that Elizabeth should follow this example, but in vain.

A fellow student of mine at Glasgow followed me to the Bar. He was a fervent Scottish Nationalist and announced to everyone that in no circumstances would he take an oath of allegiance to Elizabeth II. The Junior Lord Ordinary who was to receive him into the Bar wondered how he should handle this. He consulted the Lord Justice General, a most erudite and civilized man and a great authority on Scottish history himself. His answer to the question was simple: omit the oath, it served no purpose. Advocates are not servants of the Queen. Problem solved.

The Case of the Ill-fated Youth

The first case I ever had in court was only a few days after I had been called to the Bar in Edinburgh. I was passing by the High Court of Justiciary, the criminal division of the High Court, and, having nothing better to do, entered to see what was going on. There was no one in the court except the judge, Lord Thomson, who was the Lord Justice Clerk—one of the Great Officers of State of Scotland—the clerk and the accused in the dock. The charge was razor-slashing. The clerk asked the accused whether he pleaded guilty or not guilty. He pleaded guilty. Lord Thomson, a very experienced judge and a humane man said: 'I am not going to accept that plea. The charge is of a very serious offence and you need to take advice before you plead.' He looked around. I was the only advocate in court, conspicuous in my wig and gown. After a few words with the clerk, ascertaining my identity, Lord Thomson said: 'You are fortunate that Mr Mooney is in court and I am going to adjourn the hearing and ask him to advise you.' With that he left the bench.

Mr Mooney, aware of his own inexperience, was not so sure of the accused's good fortune but he followed the accused and the police escort down to the cells and was left alone in a room with the accused.

The accused was a young man of no more than 20, a few years younger than I, and he looked quite miserable.

'I done it,' he said, 'you can't do anything.'

'Well, never mind,' I said, 'just tell me how it all happened.' And gradually, bit by bit, I got the story out of him.

He was born and brought up in a slum area in Edinburgh. His father worked as a labourer, got his pay on a Saturday and promptly went out and spent most of it on drink. He came home late, drunk and abusive, regularly beat up his wife and any of the children who were around. As soon as they were old enough the children left home one by one. In time, Dave, the accused, followed the example of his elders but he was only a schoolboy, had no job and no money, so he stole goods from a shop with the idea of selling them and getting money for food. He was unskilled at this and arrived in a magistrate's court. It was a first offence, but the magistrate, having read the report on his background from the probation officer, decided the best thing was to send him to an approved school.

Dave served his time in the school where he found himself in the company of older boys far more experienced and streetwise than he was. When he was released he had nowhere to go and no money. He had learned a few things in the school and he again thought theft might provide him with something to live on. Evidently he hadn't learned quite enough for he landed in court a second time. The magistrate, on hearing his record, sent him to Borstal, somewhere between an approved school and prison, much stricter than the former but less authoritarian than the latter. Dave served his time again and when released faced the same question. How was he going to live? He went after various jobs but when the prospective employers heard his record he didn't get them. It happened to be autumn and farmers were looking for casual labour, no questions asked, to bring in the harvest. Dave got a job, lived frugally and saved a little money.

The job came to an end and with his meagre savings he bought himself a Teddy Boy suit, a cheap, flashy style that appealed to youngsters who didn't know better. He donned the suit and, feeling for the first time in his life that he was in fashion, he strolled down through the dock area. A group of sailors from a warship encountered him and began to jeer at his appearance. Dave's code demanded that he adopt a threatening attitude, but this only produced more jeering. Dave then tried to assault the sailors. He was no match for them. They were strong young men; he was puny. He was getting the worst of it but one of the things he had learned in Borstal was that it was useful to keep a razor blade in the visor of one's cap. Trying to defend himself against superior force, he whipped off his cap and struck the face of a sailor, slashing him with the visor. The other sailors overpowered him and the police were summoned. Razor-slashing is a serious offence and Dave now found himself before the High Court of Justiciary.

One cannot escape responsibility for one's actions but the degree of responsibility must surely vary according to the circumstances. Dave had had a bad start in life and was ill-prepared to cope with the challenges of growing up and developing into a mature and responsible person. However, the law has, in the interests of society, to ensure that certain minimum standards of conduct are maintained and the principle of deterrence requires examples to be set, so Dave went to prison from where, unfortunately, he would be unlikely to emerge better prepared for life in society. I was left with a sad memory and the thought that there, but for the grace of God, go I.

Justice is imperfect, imperfect in its systems and imperfect in the people who administer it. We need the systems and we need the people to operate the systems but we also need to keep in mind that they are not the complete answer to the problems of society.

The Case of the Kindly Juror
and the Discourteous Judge

Very shortly after my first appearance in court the clerk of justiciary, who was responsible for the administration of criminal cases in the High Court, approached me and asked me to appear for the accused in an incest case in the High Court on circuit in Stirling. The accused was pleading not guilty and had no funds to brief counsel. As the tradition of the Faculty of Advocates was to give our services gratuitously in such cases, I agreed to appear for the accused. Unfortunately I received almost no information about the case from the Stirling solicitor who was also acting gratuitously.

I travelled by train to Stirling with counsel for the prosecution, a brother member of the Faculty of Advocates, who showed me his brief. From it I learned the following facts: the accused was a miserably paid miner with little education and a very low standard of living. He occupied a single room and a kitchen and he and his wife and daughters slept in one bed. It was the evidence of his wife and a young daughter that he had committed incest with the daughter. The prospect of successfully defending him against the charge was hardly promising.

On arrival at the High Court in Stirling, I was taken by the police to see him privately. He was very nervous and regarded me in my wig and gown with alarm. 'I didn't do it, I didn't do it!' he said. I tried to tell him that I was his counsel and was there to help him as far as I could. He persisted in denying the charge. I told him of the evidence which the prosecution would produce. His wife would testify that the police called at their house to interrogate him and when they went away he said to her 'I wish I hadn't done it.' This, of course, was tantamount to an admission of guilt and would contradict his plea of not guilty. If he chose to plead guilty the judge would not hear all the details from the Crown witnesses, including the wife and daughter, and it was possible that the sentence would be lighter. It became clear to me from talking to him that he had a very limited mentality and he totally refused to say anything to me except deny guilt. Despite my queries he would not or could not offer any explanation of how the witnesses could make the statements that Crown Counsel had shown me if there was no basis at all for their allegations.

Since he insisted he was innocent I had no choice but to go into court as his counsel. The onus was on the Crown to prove the charge beyond reasonable doubt. All I could do was to wait and see what possibilities of defence might turn up. The judge was newly appointed. He was a good lawyer and, before his elevation to the bench, had had a busy practice as Queen's Counsel. He also had an unfortunate reputation for rudeness. The jury filed in and took their seats in the jury box. The court usher announced the entrance of the judge and we all stood up as he took his seat on the bench, impressive in his scarlet justiciary robes, beneath the Royal Coat of Arms on the wall above him. The clerk read out the charge and asked the accused whether he pleaded guilty or not guilty. He said 'I didn't do it!' and a not guilty plea was duly recorded. Crown Counsel rose and, according to the customary formula, announced that he was appearing for the Crown and that I was appearing for the defence. He was an experienced advocate of many years standing and was well-known to the judge. I was very recently admitted to the Bar, as was obvious from my new and very white wig, if not from my youth and general air.

The first witness was the wife who had laid the complaint. She was taken through her evidence by Crown Counsel until the point where the police arrived at the house to interrogate the accused. He had denied everything, she said, and the police went away. 'Did your husband,' asked Crown Counsel, 'say anything when the police had departed?' I knew very well what she was going to reply to that and I knew it was fatal to the defence. I rose and said 'Madam, you will not answer that question.' The Judge glowered at me and said 'And why not?' 'My Lord,' I said, 'I would like to make a submission that that question is inadmissible as a matter of law.'

I did in fact have a precedent in a lawbook dealing with the issue of a wife giving evidence against her husband. In the circumstances of the present case it was not at all a strong point and I had little expectation that the judge would allow the objection but a drowning man clutches at a straw and there was no other hope for the defence. His Lordship said to the jury 'This is just a waste of time but I have to listen to what counsel for the accused has to say on the law. I must ask you to retire. It won't be for long.'

It was not the most gracious of comments. When the jury had been taken out of the court I produced my lawbook and began to address the judge on the precedent that, I suggested, he might think had some bearing on the question as to whether the wife should be permitted to answer the question. My address was punctuated by a barrage of interruptions from the judge who was unimpressed by the precedent. Privately, neither was I, but it was my duty to the accused to put forward anything that might possibly be of help to him.

If the judge had not kept interrupting me my submission would have been very short and he could then take it or leave it. His interruptions impeded my presentation of the point and the result was to prolong the submission. At the end he dismissed the objection and the jury were brought back in. The judge was again ungracious. 'As I told you,' he said, 'the objection was a complete waste of our time and I have dismissed it.' Crown Counsel then rose and repeated his question as to what the accused had said when the police departed. The wife looked at him with a puzzled expression on her face. There was a long silence. She had remained in the witness box during the hearing of my submission. She was no more educated than her husband and had no understanding of the addresses and comments she had been listening to. Moreover, like many uneducated people telling a story, she had to start at the beginning and continue the story to the end. The dear lady had evidently lost the thread and when she eventually answered the question, the answer was: 'He said "Give me my boots, Mary, I'm going out for a walk".' The judge was furious and demanded to know why I was objecting to this answer. There was no way that I could tell him why I was objecting and I could only point out that my objection was not to her answer but to the question, whatever her answer might be. The judge was not pleased and I had to endure his expressions of strong disapproval in silence.

However, Crown Counsel was far too skilful to leave the matter there and he proceeded with his examination and the real answer came out in due course. The evidence was clear and overwhelming. There was little I could say in my final address to the jury. Crown Counsel kept his address very short, thinking it unnecessary to go over the case at length. The judge summed up the evidence which was all one-way. The clerk optimistically asked the jury if they wished to retire to consider their verdict. After some muttering amongst themselves it appeared that they did and the judge left the bench and the jury filed out to the jury room.

'Well,' said Crown Counsel, 'there is a train leaving for Edinburgh in half an hour. The jury should be back in a few minutes and I think we should be able to get that.' But the jury did not come back in a few minutes. We could not understand what they had to talk about. Eventually they filed in and the judge appeared on the bench. 'Have you considered your verdict?' asked the Clerk of Court. They had and the verdict was guilty. The clerk was obliged for the purposes of record to ask them if the verdict was unanimous. No, it was not. It was a majority verdict. In Scotland the jury in a criminal case numbers fifteen. The majority in this case was fourteen to one.

The accused was duly sentenced and Crown Counsel and I went off to the robing room to take off our wigs and gowns and other paraphernalia and don street clothes. When I came out into the vestibule it was empty save for a motherly looking middle-aged lady. She approached me and asked if I was Mr Mooney. I said I was and she added that she hadn't been sure it was me in this very different dress and without wig. 'I was on the jury,' she said, 'you may be wondering at the verdict.' I was indeed but I made a non-committal reply and she went on: 'I was the one who disagreed. You see, you looked so young and so new and the judge was so nasty to you that I just wasn't going to give him the verdict he expected. I wanted to give him something to think about!'

Juries have a heart and are not invariably rational.

I would like to say that the judge did think about it and decided to improve his manners but I cannot honestly say that he did. Had he known of this little incident he would probably have thought the lady was a fool but she was no fool.

This judge was a very able lawyer. However it is not enough for a judge to be professionally well equipped as a lawyer. He is vested with very great power and a position that is virtually unassailable. All who appear before him, as counsel or witnesses owe respect to his position but also have to take care not to irritate him or incur any negative feelings since this may affect his decisions. Good judges are well aware of all this and treat all who appear before them with the courtesy with which they are greeted. Unfortunately there are exceptions.

The Case of the Rape Which Wasn't

I was in the Advocates Library when I was approached by Ian Fraser, then Crown Counsel and one of the deputies of the Lord Advocate appointed to handle prosecutions in serious matters meriting attention of the High Court of Justiciary. Ian, who subsequently became a Lord of Appeal in Ordinary and sat in the House of Lords as Lord Fraser of Tullybelton, asked me if I would appear as his junior in a prosecution for rape to be heard in Ayr. He hardly needed a junior but I needed experience, as he well knew, and this was his way of ensuring that I got some.

I went to Ayr by train on the Sunday before the trial and established myself in the Station Hotel. Ayr was not blessed with hotels and this was the best of the bunch. Sitting down in the hotel lounge I saw that a guest nearby had a pile of newspapers and, since I had not had an opportunity to get one for myself I asked him if I might borrow one of his. My request was met with a suspicious glare and a question: 'What do you want a newspaper for?' I told him that I had not been able to get one and I only wanted a glance at it for a few minutes to see if there was any important news. His scrutiny took in my striped trousers, black jacket and waistcoat, stiff wing collar and regimental tie and he reluctantly handed me a newspaper. I then discovered that the Ayr races were on and the racing pages of his newspaper were covered with scribbled notes and figures. They were unintelligible to me but presumably had a meaning for racing gentry. My neighbour, on a second glance, looked like a bookmaker who would want to guard his secrets. Since I knew nothing of betting and odds, his secrets were safe from me.

The judge arrived the next morning in a rather grand maroon Rolls-Royce and was met by the Chairman of the County Council in morning dress. Inside, the benches were packed with potential jurors for the two trials on the list and also with the County Councillors, who had turned up in force, either to welcome the High Court on a rare circuit visit or to hear the drama of the rape trial.

The first trial was a burglary and the Clerk of Court was told by the police that the accused was going to plead guilty. The clerk asked the experienced advocate who had been briefed to defend the rape case if he would appear in the burglary case to address the court on sentence. This request was firmly refused. Counsel did not want to prejudice his client's case by appearing, with all the potential jurors present in court, for a convicted burglar. I was the only other advocate available, apart from Crown Counsel who was prosecuting, and the clerk turned to me. I agreed to act for the man and was led off by a policeman through a maze of corridors and past an open backdoor into the street to a room beside it where the burglar was waiting. I asked him what I could say for him in mitigation of sentence.

'You can't say anything,' he said.

'Oh come,' I said, 'there must be something I can say. You have a family to support?'

'No I haven't,' he said, 'and you'd better know that I have a string of previous convictions, all for burglary and I've been in and out of prison many times.'

I was alarmed. Parliament had just enacted a statute providing for lengthy sentences for persistent offenders. I told him this, but he was unconcerned. 'Can I say that you repent of the crime and are resolved not to offend again?' I asked. 'It's not much help and I doubt that the judge will be impressed but I can try.'

'Well,' he said, 'you can say that if you want to but it isn't true.'

I could see by this time that I was more worried about the proceedings than he was. I left him alone in the unlocked room, with a door onto the street open and unguarded next to it, and returned to the court. I wondered if I would ever see him again but he duly appeared a little later escorted by a constable. The judge took his seat on the bench. The Chairman of the County Council rose and made an eloquent speech of welcome to his Lordship. The clerk then called the burglary case, read out the charge and formally informed the judge that the plea was guilty. The judge, Lord Keith, who soon after went to the House of Lords, knew that I was very recently admitted to the Bar. He looked benevolently at me and waited with interest to hear what could be said for the accused. I thought it unnecessary to dwell on the list of previous offences which I knew was in front of the judge. The most I could do was to refer to the new legislation and say that this was the accused's first offence since the legislation was enacted and further that the subject of the burglary was not of very great value. In these circumstances the enhanced sentence which the legislation provided for might, I suggested, seem to his Lordship to be unduly heavy. I could see that his Lordship had been expecting the usual recital of the accused's family responsibilities and his determination never to err again and I could detect a look in the judicial eye which indicated that he had noted that he was not getting this plea. He had that string of previous convictions in front of him and, being a judge of long experience, knew that the accused was a professional and was not likely to change his profession. However, he accepted the plea, referred in gracious terms to my address and gave a relatively light sentence together with a severe warning that if there was a next time the sentence would be very different.

Now we could start the rape trial.

The names of the jurors were called out. Counsel for the defence objected to two respectable ladies, whether to their chagrin or relief we do not know, but he did not want respectable matrons with presumably strict ideas of propriety adjudicating an accusation of rape against his client. The jury took their places in the jury box and were sworn in. There was still a large number of people sitting in the public benches, comprising those called for jury service but whose names did not come out of the ballot box, County Councillors and members of the public. The clerk requested all of them to leave. Rape trials are held in camera. Many people left disappointed.

The complainant was called to the witness stand. She was not prepossessing, facially or physically. She related that she was working as a scullery maid in the kitchen of an hotel near the beach. When she finished clearing up everything it was after eleven at night. Her quickest way home lay along the beach but since it was dark she was afraid to go there alone. The accused was working as a waiter and he had just finished clearing up the dining room and getting it ready for breakfast. Since she knew that he lived somewhere in the direction of her house she asked him if he would escort her. He agreed and they made their way along the deserted beach together. They came to a bench and he suggested they sit down for a little while. It was a pleasant late summer night. They sat down and he put his arms round her and kissed her and then proceeded, in spite of her protest and resistance, to have sexual intercourse with her. When he had finished he left her and she made her way home. When she went into her house, she saw her sister sitting there and she began to cry and told her sister what had happened. Her sister took her to the police station and the police called a doctor to examine her.

The next witness was the doctor. He examined her body but found no bruises or scratches or other evidence of violence. He did find what appeared to be semen in her vagina, confirmed on further examination. The fact that there was no evidence of

63

violence did not mean that rape did not occur. She did not say that the accused had uttered any threats but it could be that she was too frightened to put up strong resistance.

Counsel for the accused in his cross-examination of the complainant elicited some interesting information.

Counsel: 'How long had you been working for the hotel?'

Complainant: 'About two years.'

Counsel: 'Did you usually finish your work every day about the same time?'

Complainant: 'Yes.'

Counsel: 'And did you usually make your way home along the beach?'

Complainant: 'Sometimes.'

Counsel: 'And on previous occasions were you alone going home?'

Complainant: 'Usually.'

Counsel: 'And you were not afraid on those occasions to return alone?'

Complainant (getting the point): 'Sometimes I was.'

Counsel: 'And sometimes you weren't?'

Complainant: (No answer)

Counsel: 'Did you ever ask any of the other employees at the hotel to escort you home at night?'

Complainant: 'I don't remember.'

Counsel: 'Well then, do you remember being escorted home by anyone other than the accused?'

Complainant: 'I don't remember.'

Counsel: 'So, as far as you remember, the accused was the

only person who ever escorted you home?'

Complainant: 'Yes.'

Counsel: 'And this was at your request, not his?'

Complainant: (reluctantly) 'Yes.'

Counsel: 'Had he ever offered to escort you home or made any request to accompany you?'

Complainant: (after a pause) 'No.'

After this series of answers, the Crown case did not look so good and at this point we adjourned for lunch. The County Council had laid on a truly magnificent lunch of the finest local salmon in their splendid dining room, but counsel did not get to taste this. We were given generous glasses of sherry and stood about, waiting to be bidden by our hosts to sit down. Our hosts were in no hurry. They wanted to chat to us and enjoy the fine sherry. Unfortunately, the judge lunched alone in his own room and before the time the councillors were ready to sit down, an usher came to inform counsel that his Lordship was ready to resume the trial. Before we returned to the courtroom, a councillor asked me if I expected to get a conviction. I replied that that depended on the view the jury took of the case. 'I can tell you what view they will take,' he said. 'Juries here don't believe in rape!'

In the afternoon the accused was called by his counsel to the witness box. He was a handsome young man. His attitude in the witness box was not defensive. He gave the impression of being puzzled as to why he was there and was anxious to tell his side of the story.

His Counsel said, 'You have heard what was said by the

complainant?'

'Yes, I have ,' he replied.

'Was what she said true?'

'It was true that we had intercourse but it wasn't rape.'

'What then happened?' Counsel asked.

'She asked me to accompany her home since it was dark and the beach was lonely.'

'Had she ever asked you to escort her home before?'

'No. I had been working in the hotel for a month but this was the first time she asked me to accompany her.'

'How did you come to have intercourse with her?'

'Well we walked until we came to a bench and she suggested resting for a little. She then put her arms round me and kissed me. It was obvious what she wanted and I gave it to her.'

'Did she protest or resist?'

'No, she wanted it. It was all her idea.'

'Are you saying that the intercourse was not at your desire?'

'I don't want to boast but I can have nearly any girl in town that I want. I never even thought of this girl. I never saw her except in the hotel and I hardly ever spoke to her. We were both busy at work and I was never attracted to her.'

'What happened after the intercourse?'

'We started to walk along the beach again but when we got near her house she said she wished she hadn't done it and began to cry. I don't know what happened after that since she went up a lane and left me to go home.'

The jury were listening intently to the good-looking

young man with his frank and open expression and pleasant demeanour. The complainant, sitting near them, looked older than him, she had plain features and a sulky expression, was round-shouldered and was inclined to be overweight. Whether juries in those parts believed in rape or not, it was obvious that they were unlikely to accept the prosecution evidence in this case. Counsel for the defence in his speech to the jury did not have a hard job. My learned leader was brief and non-committal. The judge clearly did not want to waste time in his address to the jury. He pointed out that the sole question was who was telling the truth and asked them if they wished to retire to consider their verdict. They didn't. They didn't want to waste time either.

The Case of the
Ill-informed Philanderer

Mary was working in a bookmaker's office in Glasgow. She liked to go dancing in Barrowland, one of the city's popular dancehalls. There she began to notice Jimmy, who was playing in the band. He was attractive in appearance and in manner. Mary was a go-getter. She decided she liked Jimmy and became very friendly with him. They began to live together. The band didn't pay very much and Mary could see that it was a dead-end job. She got a job for Jimmy in the bookmaker's business. He was introduced as her husband and to all their acquaintances she was Mrs Jimmy. Jimmy got better pay in the business and he also learned how the business worked. He was decisive and the boss came to rely on him. However, Mary was not content that Jimmy should remain working for someone else and she encouraged him to branch out on his own. She went with him and worked with him to establish him as a bookmaker. With Mary's energy and eye for business opportunities and Jimmy's flair for bookmaking and gift for mixing and making friends the business began to flourish. The years passed by and the business prospered. They had a house in a wealthy suburb, a son and a substantial income from the business, which was in Jimmy's name.

By this time they were middle-aged and Jimmy began to show signs of restlessness. He wanted to go off on a holiday on his own. He went to Nice on the Riviera. He returned after a fortnight. A few months later he went off alone, again to Nice. Mary began to wonder. When he went off a third time she took action. She engaged a private detective to find out what was going on. The private detective had no difficulty in finding that out. Jimmy had a flat in Nice and had a pretty young French girlfriend living in it. This confirmed the suspicion which had been growing in Mary. She was not one to accept this lightly. She confronted Jimmy. He was unabashed. If he wanted a girlfriend he was entitled to have one. He pointed out to Mary that they had never been married and if she didn't like the situation she could get out. Mary was outraged by his attitude. She told him that if he preferred his girlfriend to her she would leave him but there would have to be a division of their assets. These were considerable by now and Mary emphasized that they had been built up by their joint efforts. In fact, she said, with some truth, he wouldn't be where he was had it not been for her. Jimmy told her to go to blazes. She could take her personal belongings but she wasn't getting anything else. After all, he wasn't telling her to get out. It was her choice.

Mary was advised that by the law of Scotland, unlike the law in most countries, there could be a marriage without any ceremony or registration or certificate. The Church in mediaeval times recognized that amongst the very poor a couple might feel that they could not afford to have a wedding and might just take up living together. The canon law, the law of the Church, humanely recognized this as constituting a valid marriage provided it subsisted for a substantial time, the couple held themselves out as being married and that they were regarded as being married by the community. This was known as marriage by habit and repute. This particular provision of the canon law remained, after the Reformation, as part of the law of Scotland and was still in existence. This information was music to Mary's ears. The lawyer was instructed to commence proceedings claiming a declaration that Mary and Jimmy were married by habit and repute and that Mary was entitled to an order for the division of the property held in Jimmy's name and payment to her of her fair share.

Jimmy did not accept the claim. He contended that they were not married, never had been married and that everyone knew this. So the case went to trial. Since the nature of the case was unusual, the parties were well known and there was much publicity about it, the court was crammed with members of the public as well as journalists. Mary, having no visible income now, had obtained legal aid. It was then a matter of some comment when she appeared in court dressed in a mink coat and dripping with impressive jewellery. She was obviously a lady of character and she knew how to look after her appearance. Many a man would have been glad to have such a wife. She gave her evidence calmly and clearly. She related the history of her relationship with Jimmy. From the time they started to live together they had lived as husband and wife.

They had many friends and acquaintances who all took them to be married. Even their son had not been told that they were not married until the relationship broke up. She produced various witnesses: their bank manager who testified to their joint account; their office staff who testified to her managerial status in the bookmaking business and how they always knew her as Mrs Jimmy; the secretary of a social club of which they were members gave evidence that Jimmy was a member and that Mary was admitted to the club as his wife and they were known as husband and wife in the club. A document that caused a stir in the court was the invitation card to their 21-year-old son's wedding. This said that Mr and Mrs Jimmy invited the guests to the wedding celebration of their son.

The defendant went into the witness box. He denied that they ever held themselves out as husband and wife. The witnesses called by his wife maybe wanted to help her or maybe they thought that they were husband and wife just because they were living together. How did the defendant explain the wedding invitation? 'Well,' said Jimmy, 'we couldn't very well issue an invitation saying that Mr Jimmy and Miss Mary invited the guests to the wedding of their son. It wouldn't be nice would it?' Clearly it would not be nice but that was hardly the point. Then he called one of his employees to say he knew they were not married. In cross-examination this employee was asked how did he know they were not married. 'Well … er …' He obviously hadn't thought of this before going into the witness box. Had he been asked by his employer to give this evidence? No, he had not. How then did he get to be a witness in the case? No answer. Wasn't his continued employment dependent on his employer? Yes. Could it be endangered if he gave evidence adverse to the defence? He didn't know.

He was followed by the son. The son looked very unhappy. Did he know that his father and mother were unmarried? Yes, he knew. When did he learn this? Oh, he always knew. How did he find out? They told him. When? He didn't remember. Why did they tell him? He didn't know. Was he saying that they just came to him one day and said, "Son, we are not married?" Yes. Why would they do that? He didn't know. Would there be any point in them saying that to him? He didn't know. What about the wedding invitation? Was that sent out to all their friends? Yes. There were several hundred sent out? Yes. And all these people were being told that his father and mother were married? Yes, he supposed so. Was he employed by his father in his father's business? Yes. So he was dependent on his father for his livelihood? Yes. And as the only child he could expect to be his wealthy father's heir? He didn't know. His father would not be at all pleased if he gave evidence adverse to his father's case, would he? The son looked miserable, poor fellow, and didn't know how to answer.

Counsel for the defendant had an unenviable task in addressing the court after this. You can't make bricks without straw. There was little he could say for his client and he wisely kept his address short. The judge gave judgement for Mary. Justice was clearly done.

Lure of the East

I came out of the Advocates Library at Parliament House one late afternoon after the courts rose and crossed Parliament Hall. The late spring sunlight illumined the great stained glass window depicting the foundation of the Court of Session by King James IV. It cast multicoloured flecks of light into the hall and on to the Raeburn portraits of grave bewigged judges in scarlet justiciary robes. In the robing room an attendant relieved me of my wig and gown, tailcoat and white tie and handed me my regimental tie, my black jacket, bowler hat and stick. Suitably attired in the outdoor uniform of a member of the ancient and honourable Faculty of Advocates I walked out into Parliament Square, past Saint Giles with its crown steeple, past the ancient looming grey bulk of the castle and down the Mound. The gardens of Princes Street were bright with spring flowers. In the distance the waters of the Firth of Forth glittered. Edinburgh was my world and all seemed right with it.

It was a world that, for me, was about to change dramatically but of this I was unaware. I let myself into my eighteenth-century apartment in the New Town, built by the

Adam brothers. A buff envelope was awaiting me, bearing the words On Her Majesty's Service in lieu of a stamp. The letter inside bore the letterhead of the colonial office and said that the writer was commanded by the Secretary of State to offer me the appointment of Crown Counsel, Sarawak, and requested me to reply as early as convenient whether the offer was accepted.

I had to sit down and think. Clearly this was a crossroads in life. Should I remain in Edinburgh at the Bar or begin a new life in a new and faraway world?

Edinburgh is a scenic city and the Faculty of Advocates is an integral and interesting part of it. Every morning members walked up the Mound to Parliament House, donned the archaic dress and mingled with a fascinating crowd: the grave, the witty, the amusing, the eccentric, all learned in varying degree and all united in a brotherhood. It was a close community, housed in gracious surroundings in Parliament Square, enveloped in history, inhabited by the shades of many who were famous in the history of Scotland. There was King James IV, many-talented and active, who was slain in the battle of Flodden in 1513 when the flower of Scottish chivalry perished at the hand of the English army; King James V, whose reign was no less turbulent and who, like Henry VIII of England, was favoured by the Pope with the title Defender of the Faith; the colourful and tragic Mary Queen of Scots, who was brought up in France by her French mother, married to the Dauphin, subsequently King of France, on his death went to Scotland on succeeding to the throne, and was betrayed by the Scottish nobles to Queen

Elizabeth of England, who imprisoned her for eighteen years and then had her beheaded; John Knox, a leading figure in the Scottish Reformation, who greatly offended Queen Elizabeth by the publication of his treatise "Blast of the Trumpet against the Monstrous Regiment of Women"; King James VI, son of Queen Mary, who, on Elizabeth's death, became King James I of England; Prince Charles Edward Stuart, Bonnie Prince Charlie, who led a rebellion against the Hanoverian dynasty which had taken over the throne from the Stuarts and who entered Edinburgh with an army from the West Highlands in 1745 and marched triumphantly into England as far as Derby when his army of highlanders began to disintegrate, retreated to Scotland where his highlanders came to a bloody end at Culloden, and after months of eluding the English army in the highlands and islands fled to France.

Here I was comfortable and at home. I could see a well-ordered life stretching ahead in a congenial professional community with a common ethos in familiar surroundings. Should I leave that for what was unknown? The surroundings would be very different, my colleagues strangers and the culture of the community beyond my experience. The following day I took myself off to the library to discover what I could.

Sarawak is about the size of England and is situated just above the equator on the north-west coast of the island of Borneo. Its immediate neighbours on the north-west coast are the Sultanate of Brunei and what was then named British North Borneo, now Sabah. The remaining part of the vast island, constituting two-thirds of it, is Kalimantan, a province of Indonesia.

Sarawak was the country of the White Rajahs. The dynasty began with James Brooke, an Englishman who, as a very young man, served in the army of the East India Company and was seriously wounded in the Anglo-Burman war. He returned to England, recovered from his wounds and with an inheritance from his father, bought a one-hundred-and-forty-two-ton schooner, engaged a crew and sailed again for the East. He arrived in Singapore and there learned that a rebellion had broken out against the rule of the Sultan of Brunei in the part of Brunei known as Sarawak, which was oppressively governed by a viceroy. He sailed for Sarawak and arrived at its only town, now known as Kuching. The viceroy was unable to put down the rebellion and asked James Brooke to undertake this. Brooke did this successfully and was duly appointed Rajah of Sarawak by the Sultan in 1842 and the territory was ceded to him. He immediately drew up for himself a code of laws declaring that service of the peoples of Sarawak was the paramount object of his government and ruled firmly and fairly, associating local Malays with him in this.

James, who never married, was succeeded by his nephew, Charles, who was succeeded in turn by his nephew, Charles Vyner Brooke. James Brooke had declared: 'Sarawak belongs to the Malays, Sea Dayaks, Land Dayaks, Kayans, Kenyahs, Melanaus, Muruts, Kadayans, Berawans and other tribes, not to us. It is for them we labour, not ourselves.'

This was the policy of all three Rajahs. In the constitution which he gave to Sarawak, the third Rajah proclaimed the principles of government of the Brookes:

- That Sarawak is the heritage of Our Subjects and is held in trust by Ourselves for them. That never shall any person be granted rights inconsistent with those of the people of this country or be in any way permitted to exploit Our Subjects.
- That justice shall be freely obtainable and that the Rajah and every public servant shall be easily accessible to the public.
- That freedom of expression both in speech and in writing shall be permitted and encouraged and that everyone shall be entitled to worship as he pleases.
- That public servants shall ever remember that they are but the servants of the people on whose goodwill and co-operation they are entirely dependent.
- That so far as may be Our Subjects of whatever race or creed shall be freely and impartially admitted to offices in Our Service, the duties of which they may be qualified by their education, ability and integrity duly to discharge.
- That the goal of self-government shall always be kept in mind, that the people of Sarawak shall be entrusted in due course with the governance of themselves, and that continuous efforts shall be made to hasten the reaching of this goal by educating them in the obligations, the responsibilities, and the privileges of citizenship.

- That the general policy of Our predecessors and Ourselves whereby the various races of the State have been enabled to live in happiness and harmony together shall be adhered to by Our successors and Our servants and all who may follow them.

These were noble principles, but the history of Sarawak was about to experience a dramatic change. World War Two broke out and Japanese forces occupied Sarawak. After the surrender of Japan, Sarawak's modest economy was left in ruins. Vyner Brooke was over seventy years of age. He did not have the substantial resources required to undertake the rebuilding of the country and its economy. Nor did he have the energy or the will. The war had ended Sarawak's seclusion from the outside world. The world had changed and there was no room in it for a small oriental kingdom ruled by an autocratic Englishman. With the consent of the Council Negri, the council he had to assist him in the task of government, he ceded Sarawak to Britain and it became a Crown Colony. Despite the change in sovereignty, it was still governed, as I was to find out, with the benevolent paternalism which characterized Brooke rule.

There had been very little development in the way of roads or communication. A series of great rivers divided the country, running from the mountainous interior over coastal plains to the South China Sea. The interior was covered by primary forest, millions of years old. The population lived along the rivers and travelling from one part of the country to another involved sailing downriver to the South China Sea, sailing along the coast and sailing upriver again to one's destination. There was no radio or, except in the one or two town areas, telephone communication. Little had changed in centuries. The policy of the Brookes was simply to preserve order and administer the country fairly. The changes that had taken place in the world outside had barely touched Sarawak.

The population was made up of many racial groups: Iban, Malay, Melanau, Kayan, Kenyah, Kelabit, nomadic Penan and others. Each had its own distinctive and colourful culture. Chinese were in and around the few towns. There were many languages but Malay was the lingua franca.

There was no tourism in those days. An occasional international journalist arrived in Sarawak and wrote articles on the last paradise. They saw it as a type of Garden of Eden. There were no factories belching smoke, no poverty and no beggars, the people lived simple, self-sufficient lives, peace reigned and the colonial government, consisting of relatively few officers, expatriates, appointed by the Secretary of State, and a junior civil service recruited locally, administered the country justly and fairly, as servants of the people, but maintaining an ordered society and living within the country's modest budget.

What I was being offered was a part in this government as a law officer. It was a function very different from being an independent member of the Bar and a very different lifestyle from what I had in the historic, scenic, chilly capital of Scotland. To accept the offer would be to leave a familiar and secure world and take a leap in the dark. I decided to accept.

I had seen something of Asia in India and Burma and was interested to see more. Sarawak seemed particularly interesting but a major factor in my decision was that I would be leaving my identity issues behind since I would be with people, whether the local people amongst whom I would be working or colleagues in the colonial administration, who would take me for whatever they saw in me and would have no curiosity or interest in my descent or family background.

Informing Avice of my departure from Scotland was not easy. I had had other girlfriends but none so close as Avice. Nothing had been said but it was evident that she was looking forward to marriage. She had invited me to stay with her parents in the south of Scotland. They were good people and her mother was particularly warm. I could not invite her to meet my family because of the obstacle of my identity. Avice knew nothing of me apart from my army and university background and the fact that I was Irish in origin. I could not explain my position. There was much that I did not at that time know and much that I did not understand. This was a barrier to marriage. She accepted the news of my departure with evident disappointment. Subsequently she married a Scot who was much more suitable, having the same social, racial and religious background as herself. We remained close friends and her husband accepted our friendship and both welcomed me very warmly in their home whenever I was on leave.

Sarawak Bound

Before leaving for Sarawak, I paid a courtesy call on Sir Sidney Abrahams, the legal adviser to the Secretary of State in London. Sir Sidney was affable but vague.

'Where was it you said you were going to?' he asked. 'Oh yes! Sarawak.' He paused and I got the impression he was trying to think whereabouts in the then far-flung British Empire Sarawak was and dredge up a few thoughts on it. If my impression was correct his search was in vain since he said nothing about Sarawak. He did, however, give me one piece of good advice: 'You will inevitably find, as in any organization, that you are at odds with other officers from time to time. Your function is to uphold the law and this will not always be agreeable to administrators or others who want to take shortcuts. If ill-feeling seems to be developing, don't allow it to get into writing. Go and see the officer concerned and talk it over.' This was sound advice. I followed it and had the happiest of relations with all my fellows in the Sarawak service.

Just before I set off I watched the magnificent spectacle of the coronation of Queen Elizabeth II on television, which was then, commercially, in its infancy. Before the coronation it was announced that Mount Everest had at last been ascended by Tenzing Norgay, a Sherpa, and Edmund Hilary, a New Zealand mountaineer. It was an epic achievement.

Long distance air travel, with its concomitant of widespread tourism, was also in its infancy. This was still the day of the great passenger ships which traversed the world bearing businessmen and colonial officers, students and missionaries to their destinations and back again. I sailed from Southampton in one of the ships of the famous P&O line. A representative of the Crown Agents was waiting for me on the ship and a steward conducted us both to my cabin where the representative informed me that there were others bound for the Sarawak service on the ship: three of them were administrative cadets, one married, and one was an engineer who would be in the Posts and Telegraphs Department. The agent congratulated me on my appointment and told me that colonial officers posted to Sarawak were usually reluctant to leave it when a transfer came along. I found this out for myself at a later stage.

My fellow officers were a mixed bunch. Humphrey was handsome and urbane, agreeable company. His wife, Valerie, was lively, of independent mind and stimulating to be with. Simon was enigmatic and did not give anything of himself away. Trevor was an ex-Bevin Boy who had done his National Service down a coal pit. He was open in his views but appeared naïve and immature and I wondered how he came to be chosen and how he would fare in the administration.

Trevor's career in the colonial service turned out to be short and disastrous. He was unfit for colonial administration. He did not mature from his naivety. This became very apparent to the Resident of the large province who took him into his office in a subordinate capacity. The Resident sent him off to act as District Officer at an outstation to give him a chance to prove himself. Unfortunately all he proved was that he could not handle his responsibilities. At the end of his probationary period, he was not confirmed. He had to leave Sarawak. I tried to keep in touch with him and subsequently met him in Kuala Lumpur. He had married a Sarawak girl, but he was not in good health, was living in very poor circumstances and had become embittered.

Air travel was rare in those days. Travelling by ship was much more civilized. No jetlag, a gradual change in time zones and climate, a comfortable cabin with shower and a bed to sleep in.

It was going to take us more than three weeks to travel to Singapore where we would disembark. I had a primer on the Malay language to study and a lawbook. We strode round the deck, played deck tennis for physical exercise and played bridge and chess for mental exercise. There was a ship's library, a lottery on the length of each day's run and bingo for those interested. The Sarawak group gathered for drinks before dinner and we dressed in dinner suits for this. The weather grew gradually warmer as we passed from the Atlantic to the Mediterranean and more so after we passed through the Suez Canal. At Port Said we stopped for a day and went ashore to stretch our legs. We were amused to be approached by a man who wanted to sell us dirty pictures. We declined with thanks. 'But they are new ones!' he assured us. Even so, we were not tempted.

After leaving Port Said we spent the evenings on deck, dancing to the ship's band after dinner. Each day was punctuated by meals. A peal of musical bells signalled that the sitting was about to begin. We took our accustomed places in the dining room and were handed a lengthy menu by our white-uniformed steward. The food was invariably of excellent quality and perfectly cooked and served. Restraint had to be exercised in face of so much temptation. This was an interim period in our lives, pleasant, but we were aware that we were marking time.

Apart from Port Said, our only stops were at Aden and Penang. A steward remarked to me that Aden was the arsehole of the earth. It was a coarse description but, from the few hours glimpse we had of the town, it did not seem entirely inappropriate. Our neighbour in the port was a beautiful white French passenger vessel by name *Cambodge* bound for Indo-China. At that point, Vietnam, Laos and Cambodia were French colonies and the *Cambodge* was conveying French colonial officers, businessmen and others from the mother country to these exotic lands. There were no tourists in those days.

From Aden we sailed across the Indian Ocean. The sky was brilliant with innumerable stars at night and our wake gleamed with phosphorescence as if handfuls of diamonds were scattered in it. It was a scene of wonder. The northern tip of Sumatra was eventually sighted on our starboard bow and a day later we saw the island of Penang. We stopped briefly to allow some passengers to disembark and then sailed through the Strait of Malacca, within sight of the coast of Malaya, until we reached the great harbour of Singapore, where we anchored amidst a great number of ships of all sizes. A bustle of boats came alongside. One of them contained the Singapore agent of the Sarawak Government. He collected us and our personal baggage and ferried us ashore. Our heavier baggage from the hold was to follow us later. Once ashore, transport brought us to Raffles Hotel, one of the great caravanserais of the East. With the development of travel by air, cheap fares and the consequent growth of the modern tourist industry, there is now a plethora of five-star hotels throughout the East, all of which conform to the uniform ideas of the international chains and which are difficult to tell apart. In those days these hotels did not exist. Today, hotels like the Raffles of those days do not exist. The Raffles in Singapore, the Galle Face in Colombo, the Manila Hotel and the Peninsula in Hong Kong all had a very distinctive character. All of these still exist in name but their ambience, although unlike that of the international chains, is not what it used to be.

Singapore today is transformed. At the time of our arrival it was part of the Straits Settlements, a Crown Colony with a British Governor. It was a busy entrepôt, the centre of trade for the region, with shipping of all kinds, from great ocean passenger liners to cargo vessels and schooners from the many surrounding islands, arriving and departing daily, bringing in imports and produce, much of it for trans-shipment and re-export. Much of the trade was in the hands of British companies but there was also a great deal of it in the hands of dynamic Chinese tycoons and to a lesser extent Indians with a keen eye to business. The general appearance and atmosphere had little changed from the time of Joseph Conrad and Somerset Maugham, both of whom described the Singapore scene in their writings. It was an exotic scene with churches and mosques and Hindu, Buddhist and Taoist temples mingling with banks, merchant houses, shipping offices, godowns, European-style emporia and open-fronted shops selling a great variety of goods and foodstuffs. The population was polyglot with many Chinese speaking Hokkien, Cantonese, Hakka and other Chinese dialects as well as Mandarin, the official language of China; Indians speaking Urdu, Tamil, Malayalam and other Indian languages; Malays; Bugis, Javanese, Batak and others from the vast Indonesian archipelago; and, of course there were the British, colonial servants and businessmen, and a sprinkling of other nationals from Europe and America. Malay was the lingua franca, often spoken in a pidgin form and sometimes with grotesquely mangled pronunciation, a source of private amusement to educated Malays and sometimes mimicked by Malay comedians in a highly entertaining performance, enjoyed by all, including those who were mimicked. Chinese, who were often the victims, have a notable sense of humour, as do Malays. All this is transformed today into a great modern city rivalling Hong Kong. Much of the transformation was due to the brilliance and wisdom of Lee Kuan Yew, who became its Prime Minister and achieved an international reputation as a statesman. I was to encounter him in the course of my official duties when he was still a member of the Bar in the then Crown Colony of Singapore.

We arrived in Singapore on a Saturday but just missed the little Sarawak-bound ship that left earlier that same day. We had to wait until the following Saturday when the ship was back and would sail again. There was only one problem with this. In those days there was a tight currency situation in Britain and one was allowed to take only a very modest sum in currency out of the country. Needless to say, nothing of this was left by the time we got to Singapore. No expenditure was necessary on the ship except for drinks, and these were very cheap being quite free of duty, but, even so, three weeks is a long time. I entered the imposing portals of the leading British bank in the colony, fronting on Raffles Place, the heart of Singapore, and asked to see the manager. This was naïve. No one, except the highest potentates, got to see the manager. However I was conducted to the office of a lesser eminence, who turned out to be a cheerful young Englishman. I presented my credentials as a designated functionary of the colonial government and explained my position in Singapore. 'How much do you want?' he asked, not wasting time. I didn't have any idea as to what I might need for a week in Singapore. My hotel expenses were, of course, fully met by the Sarawak Government. 'I think five hundred dollars should cover you,' he said. It sounded a lot to me and indeed, in those days it was, and more than covered my modest requirements. Without more ado he gave me the cash and said 'I presume you will be opening an account with our branch in Kuching', shook hands and we parted.

I was impressed with his helpfulness and trust. His manner stood in marked contrast to a colleague of his in the same bank whom I encountered a few years later. I was in Sibu, the second town in Sarawak, and missed my flight back to Kuching. I had to stay overnight and being short of cash went to the bank and asked for an advance of the trifling sum I required. I was brought to the English manager. Since I was well known as a senior government officer and my name figured frequently in the newspapers as representing the Crown in local causes celebres, I anticipated no difficulty. 'Have you opened a letter of credit with us?' he asked. I pointed out that I was not engaging in a commercial transaction, that the sum involved was very small and that I had no reason to anticipate that I would miss the plane. He carefully weighed up these factors and after a pause said: 'Well I will have to telephone Kuching and check on your account.' 'Go ahead,' I said. 'You realize,' he continued, 'that you will have to pay for the telephone call.' Since this could hardly exceed a dollar or two I told him that I felt that I could bear this. He made the call and reluctantly handed over the cash.

One judges organizations from their people in the frontline. From the experience in Singapore I had an excellent impression of the bank. Had my first experience of the bank been the Sibu incident my impression would have been very different and I would have chosen a different bank in Sarawak.

Various kind people in Singapore invited me to dinner.

One of them was the Crown Counsel, a brother member of the Faculty of Advocates. The hostess had evidently taken a great deal of trouble over the dinner. The table was elaborately laid, candlelit, glittering with crystal and silver and the hostess's manner was anxious and over-concerned that everything should be *comme il faut*. A maidservant nervously served the dishes. All went well until after the main course. There was then a pause as we waited for the next course. The hostess tried to cover this by inconsequential chatter, from time to time ringing a little bell. No maidservant appeared and the hostess had eventually to leave the table for the kitchen where, we later learned, she found the maidservant in a faint, overcome by the strain of trying to meet her mistress's expectations of high life!

We left Singapore the following Saturday in a small ship which carried freight and had six cabins aft for passengers. The main cargo, just below our deck, consisted of squealing pigs and our being aft ensured that we had the benefit of their squeals and their not negligible odour. The crew, which was entirely Malay except for the captain and chief engineer, did not seem to mind the pigs despite their being regarded as unclean in Islam. Our deck space was too limited for any form of exercise and our activities were restricted to our various forms of reading and, in the evenings, bridge and chess. The sun was brilliant and the South China Sea dead calm, which is by no means always the case, as I was to find out. We passed a group of islands that, we were told by the captain, belonged to Indonesia and were uninhabited. A few years later I met some

Indonesian fishermen in Kuching who had been involved in a storm which wrecked their boat and who had managed to get to one of these islands where they had been marooned for over a year. They lived largely on turtle eggs, the island being one where turtles came ashore at night to lay a hundred eggs or so each. Turtle eggs, despite tasting rather of sea and sand, are highly nutritious and these fishermen looked in perfect health when they were rescued and brought to Kuching.

On Monday morning when we arrived on deck we were in sight of land, a low coastline which, as we approached, showed palms and a forest background but no habitation. We entered a broad estuary and made our way up a muddy winding river with banks of mangrove, the same river that James Brooke had navigated in his schooner over a century before. We caught an occasional sight of monkeys amongst the mangroves. Then we came to riverine villages with houses of bamboo built out over the river. Children were swimming and frolicking at the water's edge. Very soon after this we arrived in Kuching, the capital of Sarawak.

First Impressions of Kuching

A small group of Europeans stood on the quay to welcome our arrival. One of those waiting was a short, burly figure who, when I stepped ashore, came forward and introduced himself as George Strickland, the Attorney General. George, I found out later, was Maltese, a member of a famous Maltese family, a graduate of the Royal University of Malta, with a first-class honours degree in law from Oxford. His very first question to me after our introduction was: 'Do you play bridge?' I doubt that this is an essential qualification for the office of Crown Counsel (and I was to find out that none of the other government lawyers played bridge), but social skills matter in a small colonial community. Both George and his wife were brilliant bridge players. Apparently George's wife, his usual partner, was away and he informed me that I should replace her as his partner the very next evening. He then drove me to the government rest house, a few hundred yards away in the centre of the town, where I was to stay temporarily until accommodation was ready for me.

The staff of the rest house, Iban and Malay, were welcoming and most helpful. They were, in a sense, the hosts and they could not have been more hospitable. The atmosphere in the rest house was convivial. In the evenings, some of the secretariat confidential secretaries, all Australian, would drop in for drinks and dinner, as would some bachelor officers.

Kuching was a small town with a population of about 30,000. The Sarawak River flowed through it and there was no bridge to connect the two banks. Sampans—small canoes with the paddler standing at the rear—plied to and fro across the river from early morning until late at night. The left bank was lined with Malay villages that reached out into the river with houses built on piles over the water. Small children played on the unfenced verandahs or in the river itself. In the middle of the Malay kampungs stood a white fort, Fort Margherita—named after the wife of the second Rajah and now inhabited by the Commissioner of Police—which was surrounded by the police training school. Further inland was the camp of the police Field Force consisting of Ibans and other interior peoples: Kayans, Kenyahs and Kelabits. A little further along the river was a long low building with spreading eaves, fronted by a large lawn that sloped down to the water's edge with a formal arch and steps leading into the water. A sampan with a yellow roof was moored at the foot of the steps. Yellow is the Malay royal colour and in past days no one other than the ruler was allowed to use it. The building was the Astana, the Malay word for palace, and it had been the seat of the Rajahs and was now the residence of the Governor of Sarawak. Behind the Astana were a few government houses including the house where I would live.

The right bank was very different in character. Government launches as well as the usual Chinese launches thronged the bank. On the waterfront were quays backed by large godowns, where imports from Singapore were unloaded and goods for export, mostly pepper at that time, were stored before loading onto ships. Behind these storage godowns was the town. Small streets housed Chinese shops, markets, businesses, picturesque Chinese temples, the Anglican cathedral, a century-old ironwood building, the Catholic cathedral, two mission schools, Chinese schools and the lone government school.

The secretariat, the centre of government, where my chambers were, faced the river but was set back from it. Built on piles as a square surrounding an interior lawn, it was single storey and open on all sides with a broad verandah running the length of each side. There were no windows, only shutters, which were kept open when the office was occupied for light and to allow air to circulate. There was no air-conditioning in those days. Staircases led up onto the verandah and it was open to the public, who could call on any offices at any time. So government was open in more senses than one. The colonial government kept up the Brooke tradition of accessibility and approachability. I found this out on my first morning in the office when I paid a courtesy call on the Chief Secretary. He was engaged when I arrived and outside his office sitting on a bare wooden bench was a colourful personage dressed in a loincloth, a woven rotan hat with feathers, leopard's teeth through his ears, a bead necklace round his neck and bangles on his arms and wrists. I joined him on the bench just as the Chief Secretary emerged. He looked at us and said to me: 'Welcome to Sarawak. I hope you will excuse me for a while. This gentleman has been waiting to see me.' The Chief Secretary then addressed the visitor in Malay and led him into his office. This was the style of the Sarawak government. I was a senior officer but the gentleman who had come from the interior took priority since he had arrived before me and he was one of the people we were serving. This was a useful lesson for me. Evidently the Brooke principles were still being followed.

I had, of course, to be introduced to numerous other government officers with whom I would have dealings. The expatriate community was small and consisted of government officers and a few representatives of merchant houses. I did not have to pay a call on the Governor since an invitation to lunch with him at the Astana on the following Saturday awaited my arrival. I had a telephone call from Lady Williams, the wife of the chief justice, saying that she wanted to invite me to dine but I was not officially within their ken until I had called and signed their book so would I please do that. I remedied this omission promptly and was rewarded with an elegant invitation card. Lady Williams was very elegant as well as being a warm and generous person and the perfect hostess. They had come from Hong Kong where Sir Ernest had been a judge and had brought with them Chinese servants including their cook who, I was to find out, produced superlative dinners under his mistress's directions. The cuisine at the Astana, as I was also to find out, was not in quite the same class. The

Governor, Sir Anthony Abell, was a bachelor who had spent his previous service in Africa. He had no great interest in food and the lunches and dinners he gave were adequate but undistinguished. Simple Malay food, clearly chosen as well as prepared by the staff, was served at his private lunches and dinners.

I had been learning Malay from a textbook on the voyage over. Now I had regular conversations with a Malay magistrate, who, like everyone I met in Sarawak, was warm and friendly. My command of Malay rapidly developed and in the course of our conversations I also learned much about Malay culture, traditions and ideas. Politeness and courtesy were the hallmark of all the Malays I met and indeed, with cultural differences, were characteristic of the other races in Sarawak. Malays were Muslim but this was never a barrier of any kind. When I came to have my own house, beside Kampong Astana, the Malay village beside the palace, I acquired many friends there and was invited to all the village celebrations and religious festivals. Indeed on more than one occasion when the Koran was being passed to each of the leading guests to read a passage, it was presented to me, the only non-Malay present and known not to be a Muslim, to commence the readings. Fortunately I had by that time familiarized myself with the opening verses in Arabic of their holy book and could make this modest contribution.

My house, a single-storey house of Bornean ironwood, dating from early in the Brooke period and standing on piles like all Malay village houses, consisted of a bedroom with attached bathroom, an empty room which I used as a dining room and a sitting room. All of these were very large. The bedroom had a large mosquito-proof cage with a bed inside it. The sitting room ran the full breadth of the house with shutters all round as windows, open except in storms. Steps led down to a broad lawn which fell steeply into woodland. The view from the front of the house to the far distant horizon was of forest. A wide corridor led out of the centre of the sitting room past the bedroom on one side and the dining room on the other, to double doors at the back with steps leading down to the kitchen and servant's quarters. All round the back was a thick wood with a fringe of magnificent tall tulip trees. A rough track led from the back steps uphill to a road coming from the police training school, my nearest neighbour, and gradually descending through the village to the river.

After moving in, I had a call from a Malay gentleman, a retired policeman, living in the village to inform me that if I required a maidservant, one of his daughters was willing to serve. Yut arrived the next day, chaperoned by her sister. Her sister chaperoned her every day thereafter until, I presume, they were satisfied that I could be trusted to treat Yut with respect. She did not require accommodation since she lived only a few minutes away. She proved to be an excellent servant, quiet and unobtrusive. She kept the house in immaculate condition. The wooden floors gleamed with polish. She produced superb Malay food for lunch and dinner. Rice, of course, was the staple. I had never eaten rice except for rice pudding when I was a schoolboy and, unsweetened, it seemed uninteresting at first but this soon ceased to be the case. There are several varieties, some fragrant and some darker in colour and of distinctive flavour, all palatable and very suitable as the basis for a meal or, for that matter, eaten alone, although usually there was an accompaniment of vegetables or chicken or fish. There are different words in Malay for rice, according to whether it is the growing crop, the grain or the cooked rice. In the Iban language there are many more words since there are different words for each stage of its growth. Bacon, pork and ham were, of course, taboo since Yut was Muslim. Indeed I have never had them since and lost all taste for them. Meat was also taboo unless halal, that is, slaughtered according to Muslim custom. This was no loss since I rarely ate meat.

My daily routine was to leave the house after breakfast through the back door, which was the more convenient entrance and exit since the track leading to the road began and finished there, walk up to the road and then down past the village houses on either side to the riverbank where a government sampan was waiting to take me across the river, and walk from the little jetty on the other side to my chambers a few yards away. I came back for lunch and then returned until evening when I came home. The small expatriate official community frequently entertained each other in the evening. Since they all, with the exception of one or two, lived on the town side of the river, I had to return to the river, signal for a sampan to take me across and signal again when I was coming home. If my return was late, there would be no sampan at the jetty. The sampans would be moored in the centre of the river for the night and I had to call out and hope that one would respond and take me across. One was always good enough to do this. I had imported a small car from Singapore, which was housed at the jetty on the town side, available to transport me wherever I needed to go in town. There were only two roads going out of town. One led to a small township, Serian, then ended in Bidayoh country, about an hour's drive away over a narrow road. The other led to a point further upriver where there was a car ferry and the road continued on to Bau, another small town in Bidayoh country. When I had some free time I would drive out of town and leave the car and walk to Bidayoh villages and visit some of their houses and also climb the picturesque mountains clothed in virgin forest. One had to expect leeches but it was a small price to pay for the experience of being surrounded by the grandeur and dignity of the great trees in forest thirty million years old.

Many expatriates had a horror of leeches but, like everything else, one could get used to them. The common leech was brown and would surreptitiously attach itself to our footwear and climb up in search of bare skin. They attach themselves, inject an anti-coagulant and suck blood until satiated when they fall off, fat with blood. The sucking can last from half an hour to two hours. Another species, green with a handsome red stripe, announced itself with a bite painful enough to alert us to its presence. Removing them was best achieved with a flame from a match or a sprinkling of salt. Carrying neither matches nor salt, I simply pulled them off my skin against the advice of those who said it left attached the head of the leech and this could turn septic. In my experience it never did.

In my chambers files from various departments of the secretariat would arrive with requests for advice of how to deal with situations or advice on drafting letters or regulations, letters from District Officers and Residents also seeking advice, and investigation papers from the police on serious (and sometimes not so serious) crimes seeking directions. The directions could be for further investigation or take no further action. If they were directions to prosecute, it might be necessary to frame the charges if these were not routine. If the matter was serious and required prosecution I would frame the charges myself and notify the police that I would prosecute personally.

Every profession tends to induce certain characteristics in its practitioners. I came to notice this in the Head of the Special Branch, the branch of the police concerned with security and the connected intelligence work. He would not write to me. He came personally and possessed an air of stealth as if he suspected that he was being followed or overheard, although neither was in the least likely. He could see something sinister in everyday events that seemed to me quite ordinary. I suspected he had been too long in his special branch role. However, he was obviously very conscientious and if he was at times over-suspicious, he could take no legal action without authority. The Attorney General had delegated all his powers as public prosecutor to me.

The Case of the Verbose Counsel

My first appearance in court in Sarawak occurred a few days after my arrival. Two Ibans had been charged with and convicted of murder in the oil town of Miri. They had been sentenced to death and had appealed. It fell to me to appear for the Crown in the appeal. I studied the record of the evidence and the judgement. The essential feature of the crime of murder is that there has to be wilful intent to kill. A careful scrutiny of the record revealed no such intent. The accused persons had brutally assaulted the deceased and left him lying but there was no evidence that they intended to kill him or that the injuries inflicted would, in the ordinary course of events, have resulted in death. The Judge had erred in convicting of murder.

I went along to the Court of Appeal which was in the secretariat building. The chief justice was presiding and there were two other judges. Counsel for the appellants was an elderly member of the Bar from Singapore. He informed me that his address would take two days. 'Do you think that is necessary?' I asked and received a withering look in reply. He addressed the court at quite unnecessary length, in a repetitious address, laying undue stress on what was obvious. The court listened with patience and in silence. The facts were clear and there was nothing much to argue about. When counsel concluded his address he sat down and leaned towards me and said, 'Laddie, you've learned a lot today!' I thanked him for the benefit I had received and then rose. The chief justice said: 'You are not intending to support the conviction, Mr Crown Counsel, are you?' I replied that the Crown did not intend to support the conviction for murder but that, if it pleased the court I would address it briefly on the facts and the law which their Lordships might think indicated that a conviction for culpable homicide not amounting to murder might be appropriate. The chief justice said that he considered this a very proper attitude on the part of the Crown and the appeal proceeded accordingly.

Counsel for the accused was unfortunately not prepared for this turn of events although the facts clearly revealed what in England is called manslaughter. However there was nothing he could have said anyway and the court quashed the murder conviction and substituted a conviction for culpable homicide.

Formidable
Opponents in Court

Life in court over the subsequent years was never dull. David Marshall, who became Chief Minister of Singapore after its independence, was then at the height of his fame as the leading criminal lawyer in Singapore and Malaya. I encountered him in many criminal trials and appeals in Sarawak. He fully deserved his reputation. He prepared his cases meticulously. Every fact was at his fingertips and he had thoroughly mastered the relevant law. He was flamboyant in nature and given to rhetoric. I remember him saying in an appeal: '... and suspicion settles, like a cloud of atomic dust, over the prosecution witnesses'!

He could have made a name as an actor. In one appeal he accused me, in his address to the Court of Appeal of being not the prosecutor but 'a persecutor in the court below'. The chief justice intervened and said that he was not entitled to say this and that the case for the Crown had been very fairly presented. 'I withdraw that statement at once, my Lords,' said David. 'My Lords are aware that presenting an appeal where there has been a death sentence is a heavy burden and in the stress of the moment I was carried away.' He turned and gave me a broad wink. 'My learned friend is the essence of fairness.' David always knew how to win the favour of the court. He was well aware of Sigmund Freud's dictum that emotion influences the intellect to deliver an inference desired by emotion and not by the dictate of reason and logic. David was in his element in court. He loved it and it was always a pleasure to have him as an opponent. He was invariably courteous and, although histrionic, he was scrupulously fair with the facts and the law and never was guilty of misleading the court. He was an outstanding advocate and lawyer.

Another formidable opponent was Lee Kuan Yew. He was then in the Singapore Assembly, the pre-independence parliament where he was a leading speaker, criticizing the colonial government—never with abuse but with corrosive irony and rapier wit.

Like David Marshall, as counsel he was always thoroughly prepared. Unlike David he was never histrionic but presented his client's case most persuasively with cool and inexorable logic. Had he not abandoned the Bar for politics he would undoubtedly have made a great name for himself as an advocate. He had a brilliant intellect and his presentation was quite flawless. However, he made a greater name for himself in politics and gained a well-earned reputation as a statesman. He transformed Singapore from what it was when I first saw it—hardly different to the city known to Joseph Conrad and Somerset Maugham—and saved it from going Communist by strenuous efforts to win over the hearts and minds of its citizens and built it into the very modern, prosperous city-state that it now is.

True Judicial Temperament

Police investigation papers were delivered to me concerning a killing by four persons. I framed charges of murder against the four and a hearing was fixed by the High Court at the district headquarters at Saratok. This entailed travel by launch down the Sarawak River from Kuching and into the South China Sea, then north-east along the coast to the mouth of the Saribas River followed by a journey upriver to Saratok. My office telephoned the office of the Director of Marine to requisition a government launch. The director enquired whether, in order to save two launches going off for several days, I would be agreeable to travel in one launch with the judge. The judge had been consulted and had agreed. I had no objection to this measure of economy.

On the night of my departure, I drove down to the isolated river jetty. The road, overhung by trees, the river, the jetty and the mangroves lining the river were in pitch darkness. The only lights penetrating the gloom belonged to the waiting launch. A Malay sailor came ashore and collected my bags and I followed him on board and to my cabin. The master of the launch, a cheerful bright-eyed Malay came and presented his compliments in polite Malay. He informed me that the judge was sitting on the foredeck and was waiting for my arrival. We then cast off and the launch moved out into midstream and proceeded downriver in the darkness with a searchlight illuminating the river and its banks. I went forward and found a gentleman dressed in a loose Malay shirt and sarong, sitting at a table with a bottle of whisky, two glasses and a jug of iced water on it. I was taken aback by his dress. I didn't, at that early stage of my sojourn in Sarawak, expect an English judge to be dressed in Malay dress. What I didn't know at the time was that this judge had been a District Officer under the Third Rajah. He had been taken prisoner when the Japanese Army arrived and spent three years in prison camp in conditions of great hardship. He had a Cambridge law degree, was a member of the Inner Temple, was fluent in Malay and Iban and was very familiar with the customs and ways of the people.

However, having been taken aback by his dress and then by the whisky, which he courteously offered to me, I was even more taken aback when he began to talk about the case. He told me that, in his District Officer days, he had known the first accused, a notorious rogue. I was not happy about the judge discussing with the prosecutor the history of someone who would be on trial the following day and I soon went off to bed. Next morning when I emerged from my cabin we were sailing slowly up a muddy river lined with mangroves, indistinguishable from the Sarawak River. Saratok, when it appeared, was a small town on the right bank. Since there was no proper jetty, we anchored in midstream and the sailors launched a dinghy to carry the judge ashore. He disembarked precariously at a small wooden platform and made his way up a path to a large wooden building housing the district office, the courtroom and the police station. When the dinghy came back to the launch I followed the judge.

There was quite a crowd of Malays, Ibans and a few Chinese round the building. I robed in the police station and went into the packed court. With no TV, radio or newspapers, a murder trial in the High Court was of major interest. I looked around at the crowd. Apart from the smartly uniformed police, everyone else was in loincloths or trousers, some with a singlet or exiguous shirt and some bare-chested, barefoot and wearing necklaces, bangles and rotan hats. I felt overdressed and incongruous in wig and gown, stiffly starched wing collar and bands. I also felt, under all this clothing, as if I were in a Turkish bath and envied those who were bare bodied. The temperature outside was about 30 degrees Celsius and the shade temperature little less. The judge, also bewigged and in red criminal robes which he bore with impressive fortitude, took his seat on the bench. The trial began.

It had been obvious to me when I was reading the papers in my chambers in Kuching that there was not enough evidence for a conviction of all four. I had asked the police to ascertain if two of the accused who had taken a lesser part in the crime would give evidence for the prosecution and I undertook to withdraw the charges against them. The police had informed me that they agreed to this. So I informed the judge that I was withdrawing the charges against these two and that I would be calling them as witnesses. I produced evidence of the killing and then called these two to relate what happened. I had statements from them in front of me which showed that the first accused, who was a village headman and a powerful figure, was the principal in the murder. He was the rogue that the judge had been telling me about the night before. However in the witness box the witnesses departed from their statements. The remaining evidence, which I was in a position to produce, was not enough to secure a conviction of the headman. Reluctantly I withdrew this charge also. The evidence however was sufficient to justify the conviction of the remaining accused.

Throughout the trial the judge was, to witnesses and accused alike, a model of fairness and courtesy. He made no comment on my withdrawal of the charge against the first accused. Despite his prior knowledge of the history and character of the first accused there was no trace of prejudice. The trial was conducted in English with an interpreter but as I gained in fluency in Malay and later in Iban, I conducted trials before this judge, the only judge in Borneo who spoke either language, in whichever language was most convenient to accused and witnesses, although the judge recorded the proceedings in English in case there should be an appeal.

Coming back was not without incident. We set out from Saratok at night. The current was flowing strongly since there had been heavy rain in the headwaters of the river. As we neared the mouth of the river, the strength of the current was considerably augmented by the receding tide and we were racing downriver. At this point the master of the launch came to the judge and me where we were sitting on the foredeck and reported that a sailor had broken his arm. The master wanted to stop at a large Malay fishing village at the mouth of the river where there was a clinic and a medical assistant in charge. When we saw the lights of the village, the master stopped the launch upstream of the village by reversing the engine so that we could hold our own against the current. The launch was unable to approach the jetty and remained in midstream but the dinghy was launched. A sailor got down into it and I followed with the injured man. The river was in flood and the strength of the current created some doubt in my mind as to whether we would get to the jetty or, for that matter, get back to the launch. All depended on the sailor who was rowing the dinghy. I noticed that he had not hesitated to get down into the dinghy and that he grasped the oars with cool determination.

The moment the painter of the dinghy was released from the launch we were swept rapidly downstream with the white foam of the current gleaming in the darkness. We were swept past the jetty but with energy and skill the sailor brought the dinghy close to the bank where the current was much weaker and we managed to work our way up to the jetty, a bamboo structure high above us. Villagers who had seen the lights of the launch had come to the jetty and with their help we got the injured man up on to it. We took him to the clinic where the medical assistant gave him a painkiller and bound his arm in splints. We then returned to the jetty and the dinghy and had to face getting out into the current again. The master had meanwhile brought the launch downriver from the jetty. The current swept us swiftly downriver but the sailor managed by strength and skill to get us out into the centre of the river and alongside the launch where sailors with boathooks were waiting to lean down and catch us as we went past. It was a precision manoeuvre for if we had been a little too far from the launch, the sailors would not have been able to reach us with their boathooks and we would have been swept past and, had we been too near and hit the side of the launch the little dinghy would have overturned and, the current being what it was, that would be that.

We reached Kuching in the morning and the injured man was taken to hospital and looked after by a surgeon. I went to see him next day and he was cheerful and comfortable. I had been very impressed by the courage of the sailor who rowed the dinghy. It was a highly perilous undertaking with a considerable danger of capsizing or being swamped and he could not have been blamed had he refused to undertake it. He disregarded the risks in order to aid his fellow sailor. I recommended him to the Governor for a decoration which he duly received. He well merited it.

The Case of the Uncompensated Slave Owner

The trial took place at a district station deep in the interior of Borneo. I departed from the capital at night and drove through dark forest to the little jetty out of town. The sailors took my baggage and put it in my cabin and we sailed immediately. I sat on deck in the cool breeze of our passage listening to the sounds of the forest at night. The black shapes of the mangroves on either side were silhouetted against the blue-black sky as we proceeded smoothly downriver to the open sea. Sailing in the South China Sea can be a turbulent experience but on this occasion we were met only by a gentle swell. The sky was ablaze with stars. The constellation of Orion, with the brilliant Rigel and Betelgeuse, was high in the West and Arcturus was dazzling just above the horizon. The master of the launch came to me and we exchanged Malay courtesies. At dawn we entered a great estuary and spent the day sailing upriver. The banks were lined with mangrove in the lower reaches and with forest the further we sailed from the sea. From time to time we passed small townships and as we got further upriver longhouses began to appear on the banks. For company on the river we had the occasional Chinese ferry laden with goods and some passengers, or native longboats propelled by outboard engines and near the banks solitary sampans with a fisherman and perhaps his small son. Kingfishers darted across the river and a white-bellied sea eagle soared high overhead on a thermal.

We arrived at the station the following evening and tied up at the jetty. There was a huddle of ferries and longboats along the banks. In the bazaar there was a throng of people from upriver selling their produce and buying goods from the shops in a babble of languages. There were a number of Chinese restaurants in the bazaar, which would have provided an excellent meal in simple surroundings, but I preferred to dine aboard where it was quiet.

After dinner the quartermaster came and said that someone wanted to see me. An elderly Iban gentleman was brought aboard. He was dressed in a rotan cap, tattoos, a brief loin cloth and little else. He greeted me with serious politeness, laid some eggs wrapped in cloth in front of me and informed me that he was the father of the accused person who would be on trial for murder and had come to discuss the trial which was to take place the following day. I handed the eggs back to him and told him that this was not open to discussion. He looked disappointed and went ashore. A little time later he came back carrying a cock which he wanted to present to me. I declined this sternly. He heaved a sigh, delved into his loincloth and produced a crumpled ten-dollar note. He was shown to the gangway.

The trial proceeded the next day. The evidence was clear and the young man was convicted. The only sentence prescribed by law for murder was death and sentence was accordingly pronounced.

On emerging from the courthouse I was met by an imposing figure in a magnificent feathered headdress and leopard's teeth through his ears, wearing a colourful necklace of ancient and valuable beads, a flowered loincloth and bangles on his wrists and his knees. He greeted me and, after the necessary preliminary exchange of courtesies, would have me know that the accused person was his slave and that the sentence which had just been pronounced would result in the loss of his services. What compensation was government proposing to pay him? I pointed out that slavery had long been forbidden by law but that, as this appeared to have escaped his attention, he could, if he wished to pursue his claim, direct it to the Financial Secretary in the distant capital through the District Officer. I regretted that I could not promise him that the claim would be favourably received.

The Case of the Waterlogged Canoe and the Unlucky Crook

Travel to the interior of Sarawak was not without its perils. I once prosecuted a case involving the embezzlement of considerable funds from a district office. I had been sent voluminous bundles of receipts and accounts to study in preparing the case for presentation in court. These were sent in a large rotan box and I took this with me since the documents were essential evidence in the case. Again I travelled by launch.

The district office was situated far up a river at a point even the launch could not reach. The District Officer had sent a longboat driven by an outboard motor to pick me up from the launch. I got into the longboat with my personal belongings and the rotan box and off we went. Night had fallen and we were in darkness. It seemed that there had been stormy weather; branches and pieces of timber were floating downstream, difficult to observe in the dim starlight. We hit one of these, the canoe rocked violently and we were swamped with water. We were still proceeding but at a much reduced speed. One rarely experiences the cold in the tropics, but sitting in the darkness of night in soaking wet clothes and in the wind of our passage was the first time I had shivered with cold after my arrival in Sarawak. It was late when we eventually reached the landing stage where the District Officer was anxiously waiting. He brought me to my room in his house. Its bathroom as usual was a bare room with a concrete floor and a great jar of water with a dipper for use to pour water over oneself. He had thoughtfully had some buckets of hot water prepared and supper was waiting.

The judge had already arrived and was in another room. He was prepared to start the trial, although it was nearing midnight, so that we could return the following day. The accused person was unrepresented. Was I ready? I opened the rotan box containing the vital documentary evidence. The documents were all sodden, little better than pulp and the one or two which I had been able to separate from the mass were illegible. However the judge was waiting and there was no point in delaying matters.

I entered the small lamplit courtroom, leaving behind the rotan box. The accused person was already there under police escort and the judge entered. The charges were read out to the accused and he was asked if he pleaded guilty or not guilty. Having studied all the now unreadable papers I had no doubt at all that they proved his guilt. I awaited his reply with more than usual interest. If he pleaded not guilty I would have to inform the judge that I was withdrawing the prosecution and had no objection to an order of acquittal. The accused, unaware of the boat accident and its effect on the evidence against him and that two words could set him free, pleaded guilty and so justice was done.

Loss of the Heartsease

The *Heartsease*, a government launch, set out one night from Kuching for Sibu, the second principal town of Sarawak. On board were the master, a crew of five sailors and an English government officer who had brought with him his two young sons to enjoy the sail. This was forbidden since only government officers on duty were, by marine department regulations, allowed to travel on government launches, but the English officer was senior in rank to the master who had not raised an objection.

It was raining heavily during the voyage downriver but the journey was otherwise uneventful. However, everything changed when they emerged from the estuary into the South China Sea. A violent storm was raging and the small launch experienced a turbulent voyage north-east along the coast to the estuary of the great Rejang River, which led up to Sibu and far beyond into the heart of Borneo. Once out at sea nothing could be seen for torrential rain and flying spume and the launch was pitching and rolling heavily. Visibility was almost zero and there were no navigation aids aboard the launch apart from a compass. The master knew that to access the Rejang River, he would have to change course leave the open sea and enter the estuary but with no visibility he had only the time taken from the point of his departure to measure progress by. The master changed course, but the waves grew taller and became more violent. This was because he had failed to enter the main channel and was in shallower water. The wave action was too much for the launch and it capsized five miles from land. The crew were all good swimmers and despite the darkness and the fury of the raging storm they managed to swim ashore. The officer and his sons were not strong swimmers, if they were swimmers at all. One of the sons was saved by the master who somehow, in the darkness and underneath the upturned launch, got hold of him and at the risk of his own life swam with him the five miles through the storm to land. The other son and his father were lost.

A marine enquiry had to be held. The senior magistrate was appointed to preside and it fell to me to conduct it. I interviewed the Director of Marine and was briefed on the launch and on the question of seaworthiness. I learned about metacentric height. This is affected by the design of the boat and also by the loading. If the metacentric height is high the boat is sensitive to wave motion and will roll easily and depending on the wave motion, violently. If the metacentric height is low, the boat is less sensitive to wave motion and will not be inclined to roll but, on the other hand, when it does roll, it is slow to regain its proper balance and may fail or even overturn if conditions are bad.

I interviewed the fishermen in the fishing village near the

Rejang mouth. They were Henghua Chinese, a very tough seafaring community with vessels of age-old design, thoroughly tried in the worst of weathers. No one knew more about the varying moods of the sea than they. They said that the weather on the night the *Heartsease* was lost was the worst for forty years and they did not venture out.

The master was in hospital and I went to see him. He was very depressed and felt that he alone was responsible for the loss of the vessel and the drownings. There was no weather forecast available to him and he had no warning of the violence of the storm. It could be said that his navigation was faulty but the launch lacked sophisticated instruments—it only had a compass—and visibility was nil. He was not to be comforted. I thought he should be decorated for his outstanding courage and disregard of self in saving the boy in those appalling and most threatening conditions. He gave his evidence on this in a quiet, modest, matter-of-fact manner without heroics. The Governor, however, thought it inappropriate to decorate a master who had lost his launch. The marine enquiry attached no blame to him but he resigned from the marine service.

The Case of the Missing Resident

A short time after the marine enquiry the Governor sent for me. I crossed the river in the Governor's sampan with its regal yellow roof from my chambers to the Astana jetty and walked up the sloping lawns to the entrance. Above it was the Brooke coat of arms with their motto *Dum Spiro Spero* (While I breathe I hope) and in Malay in Arabic letters *Harap Sa-lama Bernafas* (Hope as long as you breathe). A servant in formal Malay dress conducted me to a small pavilion in the garden, which the Governor used as a study. The Governor was concerned. There was trouble in Sibu, the second town of Sarawak and the seat of the Senior Resident in charge of the whole vast Rejang area comprising a number of districts. An Indian, one of the few in Sarawak, had caused a disturbance in a Chinese shop—Sibu was a Chinese town—and had smashed a large glass showcase. The Chinese felt insulted and the Resident had reported to the Governor that there could be rioting and reprisals of a serious nature against the small Indian community. The Governor had arranged for his yacht to stand by and asked me to proceed immediately to Sibu and deal with the matter. I returned to my house which happened to be conveniently situated behind the Astana, packed a bag, went back to the river and boarded a sampan which took me out to *Zahora*, the Governor's yacht which was anchored in midriver. As soon as I was aboard we set off downriver. The light was fading and as we emerged from the estuary night was upon us and we proceeded on our way through the South China Sea under the stars.

I went to the stern where some of the sailors were sitting and chatted to them. They were dressed only in underpants, enjoying the cool breeze of our passage on their bare skin. One of them I recognized as a witness in the *Heartsease* enquiry. When the *Heartsease* capsized, he had just finished his watch and had gone below to his bunk. In the darkness and confusion he had somehow managed to break open the thick glass of a porthole and escape underwater before swimming the five miles to land. I knew this from his evidence at the enquiry. What I had not realized at the enquiry was what was involved in getting out of the porthole. His shoulders, upper arms and thighs had great keloid scars. The jagged glass remaining in the frame of the porthole after he had smashed it had ripped open his flesh as he was getting out. The effect of the salt water on his wounds must have been excruciating. I marvelled again at the hardiness of these Malay sailors. He had given his evidence quietly, without fuss or drama, and without any mention of the considerable effort and suffering involved in saving his life.

We arrived at Sibu in the morning. I was met by the District Officer and the Chief Police Officer. They briefed me on the matter and the police gave me the witness statements which they had obtained. After studying these I framed the charges against the accused person. I was told that he had obtained a lawyer from Singapore and the lawyer had arrived. I instructed that he be given a copy of the charges. Then I went off to see the Resident. I presumed that he had already been briefed by the District Officer and the police so I confined myself to informing him of the charges which I had framed and that I was proposing to arrange for the trial to take place within the next few days if this was agreeable to defence counsel. The Resident was non-committal. The accused's lawyer wanted to see me and I invited him to my office. His client had no defence to the charges. The evidence was quite clear. What the lawyer wanted to know was my attitude to the matter of sentence. I told him that his client had been foolish, his offence was gratuitous. It was not a major offence but it could have led to racial hostility. The offence was punishable by imprisonment or fine or both. I did not propose to address the court on sentence since this was a matter exclusively within the purview of the magistrate. The case had no special features which required comment from me.

The lawyer enquired whether I would object to the sentence of simply a fine. I repeated that I would leave it to the magistrate, whose local knowledge was much greater than mine, to determine what was appropriate. In turn I asked him if he was prepared for a trial within the next day or two. He was happy to get the proceedings over as soon as possible and return to Singapore. I then arranged with the magistrate to hold the trial in two days' time.

When I arrived at the courthouse for the trial I found a great crowd of Chinese outside and had to get the police to clear a way. Inside, the courtroom was also full of spectators. Inside the Bar, in front of the clerk's table was a great heap of broken glass. I asked the police inspector what this was doing there. He informed me that it was an exhibit to prove the glass was broken. I asked him to remove it. We didn't need a heap of broken glass which might have come from anywhere to prove that the glass case was broken. Moreover the accused was going to plead guilty so no evidence of any kind was necessary.

The magistrate came in and took his seat on the bench. The charges were read out to the accused who pleaded guilty. I then addressed the court on the facts, explaining what had happened and drew attention to the relevant sections of the Penal Code. Counsel for the accused then addressed the court on the question of sentence pointing out what he could in justification of a light sentence. He submitted that a moderate fine would meet the requirements of justice. The magistrate asked me if I wished to say anything. I didn't. The magistrate then spoke sternly to the accused and said that since this was a first offence he would only impose a fine.

Outside the courthouse, the crowd of waiting Chinese were talking amongst themselves but there was no sign of aggression or misconduct and they began to disperse. I went to the district office and informed the District Officer of the result of the proceedings.

'Do you know,' he asked me, 'that the Resident disappeared this morning on his speed boat to visit a district downriver?

The visit was not a scheduled visit.'

'Yes?' I said. 'You are obviously telling me something.' The Resident was inclined to be pompous; he was well aware that he was the most senior Resident and on first name terms with the Governor, who attached much weight to his views on the administration of the state.

'The Resident,' said the District Officer, 'thought there could be rioting depending on how the case went. He didn't express any opinion to you on your charges, did he?'

'No he didn't,' I said, 'and in any case this is a matter for me to decide.'

'Sure,' said the District Officer, 'but he wasn't going to expose himself to any responsibility for anything that might happen. If there was rioting you could be regarded as responsible for causing it and I would have the responsibility for handling it since he was away. Everything has gone fine so you can be sure that the Governor is going to get a report which does not mention his absence and which will give the impression that his wise and capable hands brought the whole affair to a happy conclusion.'

We live and learn. The Resident obviously had a great future. He subsequently became a High Commissioner in another territory and was knighted.

Distinguished Guests

During my time in Sarawak we had a number of distinguished visitors. The first was Her Royal Highness Princess Marina, Duchess of Kent, the widow of the Duke, a younger son of King George V. The Duke had died during World War II when his plane crashed. The Duchess visited Kuching and Sibu and then went on to Brunei. *The Straits Times* of Singapore had sent a reporter to follow her around and write up the visits. A banquet was held for the Duchess in Brunei and the organizer allowed the reporter to attend. The following morning, however, a very worried reporter telephoned the lady-in-waiting attending the Duchess to say he would not be able to accompany the Duchess that day—in fact he had acute diarrhoea—and he asked the lady-in-waiting if she could let him have a report at the end of the day which he could write up and send to his newspaper. The lady-in-waiting told him not to worry, the Duchess had also cancelled all her engagements for the day!

We then had a visit from the Secretary of State for the colonies, the Earl of Selkirk. He was a brother member of the Faculty of Advocates but had never practised, preferring to enter politics.

His Royal Highness the Duke of Edinburgh, the Consort of Queen Elizabeth II, paid Sarawak a short visit and toured Kuching in an open car through narrow streets crowded with spectators. The Duke was grandly dressed in the white tropical uniform of an admiral of the fleet and he wore the glittering star of the Order of the Garter on his breast.

The Commissioner-General for South East Asia, Mr Malcolm MacDonald, resident in Johore Bahru, paid several visits. He made trips into the interior and visited Iban longhouses. A photograph in the British Press of him emerging from a longhouse holding hands with pretty bare-breasted girls on either side of him caused a sensation in Britain. Mr MacDonald wrote *Borneo People*, a book on the Iban people he had met. After this was published he came to see me. He was one of those rare people who, when they are with you, give you their full attention. He asked me to form a trust for him into which all profits from the book would be paid and used for Iban charitable purposes.

Kuching Regatta

Every year there was a regatta on the river at Kuching. The entire population flocked to the river banks and there were many sampans gliding about. The major event was the dragon boat race. These boats were entered and crewed by departments of government, such as the post office, customs, the police and semi-official bodies such as the electricity company. The Governor had a dragon boat which was crewed by the staff of the Astana and the private secretary. The year after my arrival the Governor asked me to join the crew. So, early every morning and on some evenings we practised our paddling to the rhythmical beat by the drummer on the great drum mounted in the stern. The drumming was encouraging. It was also intended to synchronize our paddling which could be irregular.

We practised hard and we also gave some attention to our competitors. We regarded the major threat to be from the Field Force contingent. These were strongly built young men, superbly fit, all from the interior and well used to paddling a canoe. Paddling a dragon boat requires a different technique but they were out practising too and they outmatched everyone in strength and stamina.

A downriver fishing village had also entered a team. Men came from the village to town for a month or so at a time, to earn a little money paddling sampans back and forth across the river. They were black with the sun, lean and frequently seen with a cigarette dangling from their lips. We did not worry too much about them.

The great day came. The whole town was en fête and decorated. The landing steps of the Astana were well situated to view the course and there the Governor sat with a distinguished guest, the Duli Pengiran Bendahara of Brunei, the principal minister or grand vizier of the Sultan and himself of Brunei royal lineage.

At the crack of the starting pistol we were off. With powerful thrusts of their paddles, the Field Force men led the field but they did not hold the lead long. The despised fishermen, smoking cigarettes as they paddled sailed into the lead with no apparent effort. As for our boat, our synchronization came to pieces and the resulting wobbling resulted in us taking on so much water that we could not continue and we had to abandon the dragon boat and swim for the bank. The Governor was amused to see his crew, wet and dripping, clamber on to the lawns of the Astana.

That evening the Governor held a dinner party for us with Malay-style dancing, strictly men only, and I found myself with the Bendahara as a partner. My dancing, fortunately, was a little better than my paddling.

An Unusual Encounter

When the weather was good the Governor would occasionally sail downriver in his yacht, *Zahora*, and out to sea for a short Sunday cruise. He would invite one or two government officers or prominent local people to join him. On one such cruise when we were about a mile from land we espied an animal swimming some distance off. The yacht's dinghy was launched with a sailor in it. The sailor rowed up to the animal which then climbed aboard and sat nonchalantly on the gunwhale. It was a proboscis monkey. Proboscis monkeys are large in build, potbellied and have a very prominent red nose. The local Malay name for them is 'Dutchman'—not very flattering! The Governor directed the sailor to row towards the land. He did so and when he was still a few hundred yards from land the monkey slipped over the side of the dinghy and swam off. These monkeys usually live near rivers or the coast and a troop has been observed climbing a tree and repeatedly diving from it into a river. They are only found in Borneo, are very limited in number and the number seems to be diminishing. I subsequently came face to face with one while climbing through the forest of a mountain on the coast. They show no fear and are not shy. This one simply looked at me and turned away. They are not aggressive but like most wild animals they avoid human beings.

RIGHT Peter Mooney in Edinburgh shortly before leaving for Sarawak.

BELOW On the exterior verandah of a longhouse in Sarawak, the liver of a pig is being inspected to see if the omens are favourable.

ABOVE A warrior dance in a longhouse depicting the terrifying of the enemy before the attack. The parang at his waist is unsheathed as the dance develops.

BELOW A longhouse feast.

ABOVE LEFT An Iban headman. Each longhouse has an elected headman. He has no powers but acts as chairman in matters of common interest. Decisions are taken by concensus.

ABOVE RIGHT A Kelabit dancer.

BELOW A river in the Melanau district with sago logs awaiting rasping.

ABOVE Fishing with a throwing net while returning upriver after a nearly disastrous descent by raft through rapids.

BELOW Throwing the large and heavy net weighted all round the edges while poised on a narrow plank on an unsteady perahu requires perfect balance.

RIGHT
Hauling the longboat upriver through rapids.

RIGHT AND BELOW Dragon-boat crew at the Kuching Regatta.

LEFT His Royal Highness the Duke of Edinburgh receiving a Malay welcome in Kuching. Seated on the right is the Mayor of Kuching. (*Sarawak Gazette*)

BELOW His Royal Highness the Duke of Edinburgh paid Sarawak a short visit and toured Kuching in an open car through narrow streets crowded with spectators.

ABOVE Sir Anythony Abell, the Governor of Sarawak (extreme right) introducing the Earl of Selkirk, Secretary of State for the Colonies, to members of the Supreme Council of Sarawak (Peter Mooney second from left).

RIGHT Out sailing in the South China Sea, Peter Mooney saw this proboscis monkey swimming a mile from land. The yacht's dinghy was launched and the monkey climbed aboard and enjoyed a ride halfway back to shore. The proboscis monkey is known in Malay as 'monyet Belanda' or 'Dutchman'.

LEFT Peter Mooney in uniform receiving the rank of Dato' Bergelar (Dato' DiRaja) with the personal title of Dato' Kurnia Bakti DiRaja from His Royal Highness the Sultan of Selangor. The investiture was held at the royal palace in Klang, Selangor.

BELOW Peter Mooney in Scotland, 2010.

Adventure into the Interior

I had begun to learn Malay from textbooks on the voyage over from Britain and once in Kuching I obtained the assistance of a Malay teacher and took every opportunity to converse in Malay. The majority race in Sarawak at that time was Iban but when I arrived there was no textbook on the Iban language and no Iban dictionary. I managed to pick up some Iban and quite early on decided that I should make an effort to become fluent. I raised this with the Chief Secretary who was enthusiastic and agreed that I should take leave to go off into the far interior for total immersion in the language.

Wan Sadi, the magistrate who had been helping me to develop fluency in Malay conversation, was a very gentle soul, the epitome of courtesy. He had heard that I was going deep into Iban territory and was concerned for my safety. He came to warn me that Ibans were unrepentant headhunters. If I must go I must take care never to walk in front of them since I could lose my head. It was true that in the past Ibans had been headhunters and the evidence of this was plainly visible in many longhouses. Times had changed though and I had met many Ibans and had been in Iban districts on many occasions without any idea of danger or reason to fear losing my head. Dear Wan Sadi was a kind elderly gentleman but he was unduly timid and I paid no attention to his well-meant advice

Wan Sadi was far from timid on the bench however. The assistant Financial Secretary was once charged before him with the offence of exceeding the speed limit. The officer concerned was outraged that he, a senior officer of government, should be charged on the evidence of two mere police constables and be brought to court before a magistrate far below him in the hierarchy. He was even more outraged when Wan Sadi convicted him and fined him heavily. He came storming into my chambers, loud in complaint. I asked him what he expected me to do. If he objected to the conviction or sentence, he well knew the remedy. It was open to him to appeal to the High Court. He departed and did just that. The judge, who later became the Chief Justice of Hong Kong, listened patiently to the address of the appellant. In the first place, the magistrate had accepted the testimony of two mere police constables and rejected the testimony of a senior, highly educated government officer who had been a magistrate in his District Officer days and well knew the law and the obligation to observe it. In the second place the sentence was indisputably about three times what was usually given for a fairly trivial offence. All this was the subject of a lengthy address with observations on the necessity of a trial being fair which, plainly, according to the appellant, this one had not been.

The judge heard this eloquent and moving address. He informed the police prosecutor that a reply was not required.

He thanked the senior officer for his illuminating speech but saw no reason to differ from the verdict of the learned magistrate. As for the sentence, he quite agreed that it was considerably heavier than was usual. However the appellant was, as he himself had emphasized more than once in his speech, a senior officer of the government. That being the case, he could, in his conduct, be expected to set an example to all. No doubt the magistrate had taken this into account in passing sentence and he was right to do so. Appeal dismissed.

I took with me on this venture into the interior a Kenyah, La'ing Along. He had just finished his contract to serve in the Field Force and he came from the far interior and would be at home in the great forest. He was gentle and had beautiful manners like most Kenyah, spoke fluent Iban and had the renowned Kenyah skills in singing ancient Kenyah lays and dancing the warrior dances which were a feature of longhouse festivals in the interior.

I stocked up some boxes of food and, on the advice of a much-travelled friend, took a bottle of whisky which I did not intend to drink myself but which I was told might come in useful.

We sailed to Sibu where the Chief of Police suggested that I should take two of his Iban Field Force men as an escort. I did not feel any need for an escort but took them for conversation when we were on our own, which rarely happened. I had a government launch at my disposal to take me up the great Rejang River to the mouth of a tributary, the Katibas. The tributary led far into the interior and my intention was to ascend it until, on reaching the watershed, we could no longer go by water. The aim would then be to trek over the mountain barrier into another river system. I had notified the District Officer of that other region and asked him to arrange that I should be met in the headwaters of the major river in it, which I hoped to descend, by Ibans who would come up by canoe from the longhouse furthest upriver and nearest to the headwaters. The Katibas had many Iban longhouses along its course but the mountain area was uninhabited and unmapped and finding the way a matter of by guess and by God.

We reached the confluence of the Katibas with the Rejang and disembarked from the launch. By prior arrangement with the District Officer a canoe had come down from the longhouse nearest to the confluence and took us upriver. There was no possibility of bypassing their longhouse. Ibans are most hospitable and in this region they would very rarely see a visitor from the outside world. They might have a visit from the District Officer once a year or so but never a senior European officer from the central government in faraway Kuching. Our arrival was expected and we were warmly greeted by the headman and others.

The longhouse was built in the usual fashion. It stood on very high wooden piles on a high bank of the river to avoid flash floods during the heavy rainy season. The floor was of split bamboo and the roof was of broad leaves. There was an exterior verandah. The interior was divided into a broad public verandah with an interior wall of wood or leaves with a number of doors that led to the private family apartments.

Married folk and unmarried girls and smaller children lived and slept in the apartments and the unmarried and older boys lived and slept on the verandah. The verandah was lively with domestic and social activity. This was where travellers were received and lived during their stay. Access to the longhouse was by a ladder made of a long log, sloping steeply from the ground to the outer verandah, in which steps had been cut. Ascending necessitated an assured sense of balance. All the inhabitants tripped up and down it with ease but for an unaccustomed visitor like myself care was required.

Hanging from the ceiling in individual small woven baskets were human skulls or sometimes smoked human heads. These were the trophies from headhunting raids which were very common amongst Ibans in earlier years until put down by the Brooke Rajahs. I had met many Ibans. They were egalitarian, unimpressed by rank or titles; to them one man was as good as another. They were courteous and considerate. They said what they thought and were as good as their word. If they made a promise they kept it. No matter their wild past, I had always found them friendly and likeable.

The men wore only a loincloth, usually black in colour but on festive occasions some young men would wear flowered loincloths. The women wore only a short skirt from waist to knee, of cloth woven and dyed by themselves in traditional patterns like their blankets. Both sexes might wear earrings of metal or bone worked by themselves and necklaces of old beads, perhaps with wristbands and, in the case of men, bands just below the knee, of twisted black fibre.

A small breed of hunting dog was usually seen on the verandah but they kept out of the way. At night, the light was provided by burning pieces of dammar, a type of vegetable gum, which gave a low flickering light. When these were extinguished and the families had retired to their apartments, the dogs were liable to approach and press themselves for warmth against those sleeping on the verandah.

After darkness a young unmarried man, after a suitable interval, might quietly open one of the apartment doors and slip inside and approach the mosquito net of an unmarried daughter, enquiring, in a whisper, if he might enter within the net. If he was allowed to, he would enter and they would converse in whispers. If he was found by the maiden to be congenial he might be permitted to go further. This was a recognized Iban custom and the parents or other inhabitants of the apartment, if they were not sound asleep, pretended to be and never interfered. There was no other opportunity for privacy. Marriages almost never ended in divorce or separation so the custom may have allowed the couple to decide whether they were suited to each other and wanted to marry.

Taking a bath, which everyone did in the evening before dark, was taken naked in the river but with modesty, concealing the private parts with a hand. The river was also the source of drinking and cooking water which was carried up the steep log access ladder by the women in earthenware pots. This was a constant labour for the women during the day. The river water was never drunk unboiled.

Roaming free underneath the longhouse were small

domestic pigs. They rooted amongst any rubbish flung from the longhouse, of which there was little. I was advised when going down early one morning to relieve myself to take a stout stick. I soon found out the reason. The pigs well knowing what could happen, followed me into the undergrowth, anticipating breakfast and were not content to wait until it arrived. The stick was necessary since they were not to be dissuaded by words or gestures.

Our arrival at all the longhouses was received as a great event. After bathing, we would settle on the interior verandah, our backs to the exterior verandah while the men of the longhouse would sit crosslegged in a semicircle facing us with the women behind them. They expected an oration from me on current affairs and matters of interest and there was then a discussion. Ibans are forthright and did not hesitate to express their opinions but always politely. The women did not speak then but expressed their views to their husbands when they had retired to their apartments and this could result the following day in a man altering the view he had given the evening before.

When the discussion was over, a quasi-religious ceremony was always held. The headman would wave a cock in the air over the principal visitor with appropriate incantations and an offering of boiled eggs would be placed on the roof of the exterior verandah, an offering to the spirits which was later consumed. The people were animists but had a vague conception of a supreme power and spirits of the forest. Their moral standards were very high; theft was almost unknown as was lying.

Then followed a feast with whatever food was available; their own hill rice, perhaps a few little fish from the river or, as a special treat, a small domestic pig slain in our honour; never any vegetables. On a rare occasion wild boar was served. I added a contribution from my store and was careful not to eat any of it but to have some of their rice and a little fish. They lived in humble style but were generous with whatever they had.

There was also dancing. An athletic young man dressed in loincloth with a hat made of skins and hornbill plumes and with a ceremonial machete and its sheath, beautifully made and decorated, in most cases by himself, would suddenly appear with a yell. He would bend, twist and turn gracefully, unsheath the machete, stamp his feet with bloodcurdling shrieks and fight an imaginary enemy, execute high leaps with perfect landings, approach nearer and nearer to me, whirling round and round with the machete inches from me. All this was performed with the grace, poise, balance and perfect judgement of a ballet dancer. I knew this was intended to entertain the company by eliciting a reaction from me but I had complete confidence in their agility and balance and judgement and had no difficulty in maintaining a calm and impassive demeanour no matter how near the machete approached. Although they had been headhunters in the past this practice was ended and there was no case of headhunting during my years in Sarawak. After this virtuoso exhibition there would then be dancing by some of the bare-breasted maidens of the house, not athletic in style but equally graceful. Then two of the maidens would come to me and invite me to perform. I would demur; I could not compete with the grace and agility of the male dancer. However the maidens would come to my side, each would grasp one of my ears and drag me up and into the centre. At this point I had to do the best I could, donning a hat and taking up a machete. It was not a wonderful performance and certainly not to be compared to what we had just witnessed but this was not expected of me. They just wanted me to join in and be one of them, which I gladly did.

One evening, while sitting on the interior verandah, we heard a commotion outside and a man ran in with some news. We quickly moved to the exterior verandah and witnessed far above an eclipse of the moon. The Ibans brought out their handwoven and hand-dyed blankets, which have a semi-sacred significance and waved them at the moon until the eclipse passed. When we returned inside they explained to me that a dragon was eating the moon and they were waving the blankets to discourage it. They did not tell me this with any great conviction and indeed asked me what I thought about the phenomenon. Our only source of illumination was dammar, a kind of gum which burns slowly and emits a gentle flame. I took one of these lights, extracted a mirror from my bag and tried to demonstrate the shadow of the earth cutting off from the moon the light of the sun. They listened politely but were not really interested.

We made our way upriver, stopping each night at a different longhouse. The morning after one of these night stops, as we were about to leave, there was some excitement outside and I saw the son of the headman, who had been an agile dancer the night before, being carried up from the river and laid down on the interior verandah. He was surrounded by people. I enquired what was wrong and was told that the young man had gone out early in the morning to his farm but had experienced great abdominal pain, due to his insides being twisted by a demon. The house possessed a dukun—a healer and magician—and he was quickly summoned. The dukun knelt beside the youth and began to utter unintelligible incantations. He broke an egg over the youth's abdomen and began to rub the abdomen with it. I managed to get close to the boy and prodded his right lower abdomen with my forefinger. The boy reacted with a physical spasm of pain. Appendicitis! I took the headman aside and told him that the boy was in danger. I tried to explain the nature of the appendix and the inflammation and the possibility of its rupture. I offered to take him immediately downriver to Sibu where there was a district hospital with a resident surgeon. The headman thanked me and said he did not wish to trouble me and perhaps he would take him downriver himself later. It was clear that this was a polite way of declining my proposal. He was unimpressed by my diagnosis and would rely on the dukun.

I had a parallel experience in a longhouse further upriver. The people knew nothing of Western medicine and let ailments and injuries take their course with such assistance as a dukun could provide. However, before I left Kuching, the Director of Medical Services suggested that I should take a first aid box. He had one made up containing tablets for headaches, fever and stomachache, ointment and lotions for skin complaints and various other simple remedies. So when I stopped at a longhouse I would tell the occupants I had some medicines and people would sometimes ask for them. At this longhouse, an old lady came to me and asked me to come to her apartment and see her granddaughter. I did and found a girl of about twelve lying on a blanket and looking very ill. I took her temperature which was alarmingly high and was going to give her some tablets for reducing this. I asked the old lady about the child's illness. She pulled aside the blanket covering the child's body and I was horrified to see her leg bloated and badly discoloured with her groin very red. I asked for an explanation and was told that she had been bitten by a snake. It was obvious that immediate medical, if not surgical, attention was needed. Again I made the offer to take her down to the district hospital. The old lady said she must wait until her son, the child's father returned from a hunting trip in the forest. She did not know when that would be. I failed to convince her of the need for urgent attention. Western medicine was unknown to the people and they preferred the old ways.

A year or so later I travelled on official business to a remote station by government launch. A group of nomadic Penan was also there as the headman of the group was required as a witness in the murder trial that I had come to conduct. He did not show up at the court and the police told me that he was at the Dayak rest house with the remainder of the group, one of whom was sick. I went to the rest house and summoned the medical assistant in charge of the government medical clinic at the station. I found that the sick person was a young girl. She was lying on a blanket in the embrace of another member of the group, a lady. The medical assistant told me that the girl was suffering from advanced TB. I spoke to the headman and said that the girl was suffering from a disease which was highly infectious and the lady should not be in close embrace. The headman said that the lady was a close relation of the girl and that they loved each other very much so it was unthinkable to expect her to separate herself. I told him that I had a government launch at my disposal and offered to take her to the district hospital in a town along the coast. He said that they knew that she was going to die and it was better for her to stay with her own people in surroundings which were not strange to her.

Hygiene and skilled medical treatment are desirable but there are human values which prevail over such considerations. Not for the first or the last time I felt that, despite my superior formal education, I had much to learn from the people I was serving.

On one occasion amongst those coming to me for medical aid was a strong young man. His entire body was covered in intricate convoluted designs, which, at a distance, I took to be a tattoo, more elaborate than customary. However, when he came close and I looked at his skin, I saw that this was not tattoo but tinea imbricata—ringworm. The only thing that I could offer him was a tablet of medicated soap, unlikely to be effective. I gave it to him and advised him to wash with it. He appeared to be offended, perhaps thinking that there was an imputation that he was unclean. I advised him to go to the nearest district headquarters where there was a clinic where his affliction could be better dealt with.

When we arrived at the longhouse furthest upriver on the Katibas I had to prepare for the crossing of the watershed. This would take some days. Since the route would take us through unmapped territory it was not possible to determine how many days would be required or what route to choose. I asked the headman if I could take a party with me. We would have to carry some food, principally rice. We had shotguns to hunt for game. Nine Ibans volunteered to accompany me and I arranged suitable remuneration for them with the headman. We set off in three small canoes and paddled upriver which, by now, was narrowing and becoming shallow. When we encountered rapids, we frequently had to get out of the canoes and drag them over as the river was not deep enough. Eventually we could take them no further. They were dragged up on the bank and left behind. We now began to trek through primary forest with great trees, eighty or ninety feet high. Their canopies were far above our heads and most of the life of the forest, fauna as well as flora, was up there. Soon we were climbing steep slopes. During our progress the Ibans were keeping a sharp lookout for game. We stopped in the early afternoon of each day to make camp and a shelter of branches and broad leaves was constructed. Some of the party went off to gather firewood and some to hunt. The hunters were hoping for wild boar which is greatly prized as a delicacy but we did not get one. We did eat sambhur deer, the flesh of which the

Ibans hung over the fire to smoke before eating. It is not a method of cooking to be recommended. The meat was tough as old boots and tasted of smoke but my companions seemed to enjoy it. Meat was a luxury for them. We also ate monkeys and some small mammals. Some of these were just placed on the fire without being skinned. The stomach burst with heat and the entrails came out. The charred fur was scraped off by my companions with a stick and the flesh consumed. I found this less than tempting and had little to eat apart from rice.

In the shelter, during the early hours of darkness we talked of all sorts of things. The Ibans spoke of their legends and traditions and I spoke of the world outside. Since there was no radio or TV in Sarawak at that time and there were no newspapers or, for that matter, schools, in most of the interior, there was little knowledge or awareness of any developments outside their own personal experience. They were intelligent, active and resourceful and they had grown up to be self-sufficient and independent in every respect and their initiative was admirable. They treated their children as equals and the children combined the charm and innocence and playfulness of the young with a surprising maturity. On a previous journey, I had arrived in the afternoon at a longhouse where the adults had left for their farms and some young boys, none of them more than about ten or eleven years old, dressed in loincloths like their fathers, had come down to the riverbank and solemnly greeted my party, led us up into the longhouse, where they served us pineapples and fresh young coconuts then sat around us as their fathers would have done, conversing gravely. They behaved towards us exactly as their fathers would have done, according to Iban custom which they were well familiar with and with natural good manners and consideration for the guests.

During our talks in the darkness, lying on the ground under our shelter, I became aware of my Iban companions' beliefs about the world we live in. They spoke of the spirits of the great forest but were reluctant to dwell on them or to allow me to talk of them. When I ventured to speak to them with stories of the banshees and other paranormal phenomena which I was regaled with as a child in rural Ireland, they did not wish to listen.

The oldest member of the party was as vigorous as the young. He returned from the afternoon foraging for firewood with a greater load than anyone else. He spoke with a broad accent, which I understood with some difficulty. I asked him his age, knowing well that his birth would never have been registered and that birthdays were not observed amongst the peoples of the interior. However, he remembered the day of darkness when the whole sky was obscured with black cloud. This could only be the day when the volcano Krakatoa violently erupted and it is recorded that the ash covered a vast area. This occurred in 1883. Assuming that he was 5 years old at the time, and he may have been older, this put him in his mid-eighties. His strength and fitness were a tribute to an unceasing daily active life.

At one point on our journey the stream deepened as it approached a bend and was too deep to wade across. The

Ibans, whose sense of balance was better than mine, decided to climb up the steep bank and make their way precariously along its sides. I gave them my gun and my rucksack and decided to swim through the pool. When I swam round the bend, I saw a crocodile, which looked to be about ten feet in length, resting motionless at the edge of the stream. It did not remain motionless. It was startled at the sight of me and moved with surprising speed into the stream. I was startled too and moved with the utmost speed I could muster out of the stream and onto the opposite bank and rapidly away from the crocodile which, I was relieved to observe, displayed no sign of wanting to follow me. I had not expected to meet a crocodile so far upriver and it was not uncommon for people to be taken by a crocodile. They could be aggressive and were known to upset a canoe to get at whoever was in it.

Eventually we reached what appeared to be the watershed: it was a pass in the mountains. We trekked up through this and then we began to descend. We arrived at a stream and followed it downhill for two days until we arrived at the confluence of the stream with a much broader and much deeper river. We could go no further without boats. This is where, if we had reached the right river, I expected to find some signs of the party that I had asked the District Officer of the area to send up to meet me. We were now on the bank of a river in the midst of the great forest. It looked as if no one had been there since Adam and Eve. We made a shelter and talked. The Ibans said we would have to go back. They had very little rice left and no more salt. We had no other food, apart from a few tins that I still had. I said that I was not for going back but for going downriver. They insisted that was impossible without a boat but I suggested that we could make rafts. They said that to go downriver by raft was not possible since there was a series of notoriously steep rapids which they had heard of. I said that we must then part company.

Ibans are very good speakers and appreciate oratory if the occasion is right. I judged that the occasion was crucial and called for whatever fluency in Iban that I had acquired and whatever oratorical skill I could command. I began by expressing, quite sincerely, my admiration of Ibans, their egalitarianism, their sturdy independence and self-sufficiency, their tradition of courage which was well known, their reliability, their honesty and their sincerity. I was truly grateful for their company and their comradeship, which I would long remember. Since this was our last night together, I had a bottle of whisky and I gave this to them to enjoy the evening. There was just one last thing that I would ask of them. I would like them in the morning to make a raft for me before they went back. They remonstrated that rafting was too dangerous even to think of. However I said that I would take my chance on that. This talk of parting and the raft resulted in an atmosphere of gloom and the Ibans moved away to where I could not hear them and began a discussion amongst themselves. After some time they all came back to the shelter where I was and said that they would make the raft and that two of their number would accompany me. I was touched and thanked them but was concerned for the safety of the two who would accompany me.

They said that I could not go alone, that I would never make it on my own through the rapids and these two would also take the risk although they were not sanguine and still advised against going. No more was said. The whisky was distributed and the last of the food eaten and we talked long into the night before going to sleep.

Next morning they collected bamboo and creepers and neatly constructed a raft with a central pillar of bamboo to which we could tie my rubber groundsheet in which were placed my few belongings to keep them dry. We had poles for steering. We said goodbye and they stood looking at us from the bank and off we went. I left behind my servant, La'ing, and the Field Force men.

Great trees overhung the river on either side and it was only in the centre that the sunlight penetrated the canopy. The forest was quiet and still. It seemed an idyllic, paradisal world. We drifted gently downstream for some time before the current became faster. We were approaching the rapids. Suddenly they came into view. The river foamed white over and in between boulders and smaller rocks. We had to make up our minds quickly which channel looked like being the safest and we tried to steer the unwieldy raft for it. Then we were into it. We fended off boulders with our poles but the raft bucked and heaved and scraped over submerged rocks and stony shallows and the river foamed over the raft. It was strenuous work and we had little control. I thought we were going to break up or, at the steeper parts, completely turn over. Although badly shaken, we managed to remain on the raft until we got through the rapids and were drifting in deep water again. But the raft was damaged and looked as if any more strain could break it apart. Moreover I was seriously concerned for the Ibans. We were lucky to survive the passage of these rapids unharmed. I did not know how many more of these hazards lay ahead but the experience of the first had demonstrated that the risk of serious injury or death was considerable. I had been very foolish to disregard the advice given to me by those with much greater experience of the hazards of travel in the interior than I had. It was my prerogative to take a risk for myself, but I would be responsible if anything happened to my two Iban companions. I had no right to put them in a situation of such danger. I was pondering whether the right thing to do was to disembark and make our way back through the forest. This would not be easy. Would the party we had left behind still be where we left them? They would not have lingered long. Making our way back through the forest would take a good deal longer than our passage downriver. If the party had gone, as seemed likely, we would have to face the prospect of journeying for days, climbing up over the watershed again and down the other side and then somehow making our way, without boats, downriver to the last longhouse we had departed from. It was a daunting prospect. With almost no food, our survival would be at stake. And so it would be if we continued on the raft. I reproached myself for the folly of having created this predicament.

As my mind was in turmoil with these thoughts, there appeared from round a bend in the river, three longboats making their way upstream. This was an enormous relief and I thanked God for it. They approached us with cries of greeting. This was the party I had asked for. They had come up some time earlier to meet us but, while waiting, had run out of food and gone back for fresh supplies. We abandoned the raft and got into the boats. We decided to continue upriver to where we left the others in the hope of finding them still there. There were large fish swimming in the crystal clear river and the party had throwing nets. These fish had never or had very rarely been netted and soon our canoes were laden with them. Our party had plenty of rice and we paddled vigorously up to where my original party had camped for the night. At the rapids we got out of the canoes and dragged them, sometimes through the rapids and sometimes on the bank of the river until we were past them. When we arrived, our original party was just about to leave. They were delighted to see us and greeted us with broad smiles and laughter. We had a feast of roasted fish and rice, and related our experience. I apologised for thinking that I knew better than them. The new party supplied the Katibas party with ample supplies of fish and rice and we exchanged warm and cheerful goodbyes all round.

The rapids on the way downriver were indeed a hazard but longboats are much more manoeuvrable than a raft and our intrepid and skilful Iban paddlers brought us safely through them although there were still some perilous moments. The Katibas party had been right. We would never have made it on the raft. I was indeed foolish to think that I knew better.

When I eventually got back to Kuching I had been speaking, hearing and thinking nothing but Iban day and night for a month. When I began to speak to Yut, my Malay maidservant, I had a mental block and instead of speaking Malay I found myself, to her astonished incomprehension, speaking in a stream of Iban.

A Nocturnal Visitor

My house was lonely and isolated, surrounded by trees and with a rough road leading to its back entrance. The village of Kampong Astana was my nearest neighbour. The villagers told me that a pontianak, an evil spirit which took the form of a beautiful woman, lurked around my road. The pontianak would appear to a young man and lure him into the trees, never to be seen again. Perhaps I was unattractive to the pontianak for she, or it, never appeared to me. Nor did she appear to anyone else that I met.

When I returned from the Katibas, La'ing was still with me and I invited him to stay for the night before beginning the long journey into the interior back to his home village. It was late and after a simple meal we retired. La'ing slept on his sleeping mat in the bedroom. I switched off the lights and was just about asleep when I heard a knocking on the wooden wall. I switched on the light and La'ing sat up. The knocking was brief and was not repeated. I bade La'ing sleep and I switched off the light again. But before I fell asleep, I suddenly heard the back doors, never locked, flung open and the sound of someone wearing boots walking along the corridor and into the sitting room. Angry at the intrusion, I snatched the ornamental parang hanging by my bed and rushed out into the corridor. A glance to the right showed me the open doors; I turned left and entered the sitting room, switching on the light. To my surprise it was empty. I could not believe it and looked behind, and even under, the furniture. The room was certainly empty. Yet I had not heard the footsteps go out again. Very odd! I went back, closed the doors and returned to my bedroom. By now La'ing was sitting bolt upright and was very alarmed. I bade him sleep again, switched off the light and went back to bed. A few minutes later, again I heard the sound of the back doors being flung open and the sound of boots on the wooden floor passing along the corridor and into the sitting room. I immediately snatched up the parang again and went into the corridor. This time I closed the back doors first. Now I have him, I thought. I went into the sitting room and switched on the light. It was empty!

I picked up the telephone which was connected to the switchboard of the police training school and was connected by it to the guardroom. I asked the guard commander to find the sentry who was on patrol at night and included my house on his beat. I asked the guard commander to bring the sentry to me. The only explanation that I could think of for this unprecedented intrusion was that the sentry had entered the house: this would explain the sound of boots—no one else wore boots and as was the custom, anyone entering the house took off their shoes. The guard commander arrived with the sentry. I asked where he had found him, thinking that if he was the intruder he would have been near the house when the guard commander found him. However he had been at the other limit of his patrol. It was obvious to me that neither of them had any idea of why they were being summoned to see me at such a late hour.

Next morning, the commandant of the police training school, who had received a report from the guard commander, telephoned me to ask if anything was wrong. I explained. He told me that the guard commander and the sentry had come to their own conclusions as to the mysterious summons and the story had now gone round the school that the ghost which everyone suspected must be around this lonely house had manifested itself that night. And soon, of course, it spread around Kampong Astana and from there made its way into the town.

I recalled that the previous occupant of the house, a senior police officer, told me that he stabled his two horses behind the house. On more than one occasion the horses had become very agitated in the middle of the night. The noise they made aroused him from sleep and he had to go out and pacify them. He never did discover the cause of their agitation.

I thought my friends might be reluctant in future to accept my invitations, to face, in the darkness of the night, the rough, lonely road with its lurking pontianak and dine in a ghost-ridden house. On the contrary, they were delighted to come to the haunted house and hear the story first hand.

The nocturnal visitor came once more. At Christmas the Governor held a dinner party at which I was a guest. The dinner was followed by dancing and I left the Astana only a short time before dawn. On entering my house, I sat in the sitting room since my mind was too full of the events of the celebration and I had no desire for sleep. I did not switch on the light and was sitting in the dim starlight from the windows when suddenly I heard the sound of the back doors being flung open and the sound of someone in heavy boots coming along the corridor. I could not see into the corridor from where I sat but I waited with interest to see what would emerge from the corridor. The sound of the boots ceased and nothing emerged. I went to look down the corridor and, sure enough, the doors at the end had been flung open. They were heavy doors and there was no wind.

My house had a history. During the Japanese Occupation it was occupied by the Kempeitai, the notorious Japanese military police and the villagers had told me of the tortures and killings that took place there. Also, near my house was the place where execution of criminals took place under the Rajahs. A grave was dug and the condemned man was brought there and asked to sit by the grave. He was then given a cigarette to smoke and while he was doing so the executioner came from behind and stabbed him behind the left collar bone with a naked keris into the heart with the result of instant death.

The nocturnal visit was not the only psychic experience that I had in Sarawak. I was conducting an enquiry before a magistrate into the large amounts of petrol that were disappearing from a public works department store. As the enquiry proceeded, suspicion began to focus more and more on a particular PWD officer. On the day the evidence concluded, the magistrate adjourned until the following day when he would deliver his findings. It seemed to me then that there was sufficient evidence to order next day the arrest of the officer on charges of criminal breach of trust. The officer concerned had been in court throughout and had heard the evidence, but I had not talked to him. During that night I woke up and found myself standing in the middle of the deserted village road with, for some minutes, no idea of where I was or who I was. Realization dawned but I had no consciousness of how I had risen from bed and made my way to the village road. Next morning I attended the court to hear the magistrate's findings. As he was delivering them, a police officer came to me and told me that the suspect, who was not present, had been found at his house where he had hanged himself during the night.

The Case of the Trading-boat Murders

On some rivers enterprising Chinese would load a boat up with supplies and go trading upriver, stopping for a day or so at longhouse jetties, trading their goods for whatever the longhouse inhabitants had to offer—hill rice, dammar, rotan, woven blankets of vegetable fibre tie-dyed with natural dyes. On the hull of the boat there would be a long wooden cabin with stout wooden doors housing the trader and his goods.

It was on one of these boats that a trader and his wife arrived at the jetty of a longhouse and spent the day trading. They retired for the night and shut the doors. Some hours later when all was quiet and the longhouse was asleep, two young men from the longhouse came down to the boat and knocked on the door. The trader called out and asked what they wanted. They told him someone was sick and they wanted some medicine. The trader carried some simple medicines for headaches, fevers, stomach trouble and first aid and he opened the door. The two young men rushed in, broke the arms and legs of the trader and his wife then smashed in their skulls. They took what they wanted, doused the bodies with kerosene and set them on fire.

The outrage was discovered the next morning and a few days later the news percolated downriver to the police in the district headquarters. No one in the longhouse knew who the culprits were. At least that is what they told the police. The police well knew that a longhouse is a tight community, inter-related by blood and marriage with strong social ties. It was unlikely that any member of the community would tell the police what he knew or suspected. Even if he was inclined to give any information, he would be deterred by the prospect of reprisals from the culprits' families.

However young men are not noted for their discretion or ability to keep their exploits secret. News began to spread in the district about two young men who, on visits to neighbouring longhouses, were dropping mysterious hints, boasting about their clandestine achievements in veiled language. The news reached the police and with this to work on, the police were not long in uncovering the details of the murders and the identity of the murderers. Once again I set off for Saratok, the scene of my first murder trial. We found the river in flood but sailed up it without mishap and anchored in midstream off the town. The jetty was underwater as was the flat land surrounding it. Fortunately, the district office and courthouse were situated on a little hill a few hundred yards from the river. Clad in my black trousers, white shirt, stiff collar and bands and black coat and carrying my gown over my arm and my wig in my hand, I got into the launch's dinghy and was rowed ashore by a sailor. I was met by a bare-legged policeman who was to accompany me to the court. I removed my shoes and socks, rolled up my trouser legs and stepped out of the dinghy. I remembered from my previous visit that there was a deep drain to the left of the path leading to the hill and I made a point of keeping to the right of where I thought the drain was. It was impossible to see anything below the surface of the muddy floodwater. Halfway to the courthouse the policeman warned me that I was straying too far to the right of the path and that I should move to the left. Well, I thought, he should know. I moved to the left and descended rapidly into the drain, totally immersed. I clambered back on to the path but had to go back to the launch with my sodden muddy clothes to change. I had no other gown or jacket or wig to change into and made my appearance rather informally in an open-necked shirt and trousers. I saw the judge beforehand in his chambers and explained. 'Well,' he said, 'you will be a lot more comfortable than we normally are.' Wearing our normal court dress was archaic, alien, quite inappropriate and bizarre in the tropical heat of a non-airconditioned courthouse amongst people either bare-bodied or wearing light cotton shirts. Justice can be done with dignity without the paraphernalia reflecting the cultural history of a distant and very different country.

The evidence in the case was clear. I addressed the assessors at the end and explained that on a charge of murder the Crown had to prove that the two accused killed the boat-hawker and his wife and, further, that they intended to kill them. The evidence of the killing was uncontroverted. As for intention, what could be the intention of the accused in breaking the arms and legs of the victims, smashing in their skulls, dousing them with kerosene and setting fire to them? The assessors were an Iban Anglican clergyman, who subsequently became a bishop, and a young Scot who was working in an Iban development scheme upriver. The latter sat crosslegged on his chair on the bench. He was dressed in a shortsleeved shirt open to the waist, a pair of shorts and nothing else. Throughout he picked his teeth with a toothpick. Later I learned that the toothpick replaced the cigarette which was habitually between his lips.

The judge summed up to the assessors briefly and confirmed my address. We then adjourned for the assessors to consider their verdict. During the adjournment I had a talk with the Chinese headman. He informed me that the young Scot had, as sometimes happens to impressionable people of limited culture, become a complete Iban in speech and habits and identified himself totally with Ibans. He wondered what sort of verdict he would pronounce in a case where the accused were Ibans and the victims were Chinese. I assured him that there could be only one verdict in this case. However the headman was right in his forebodings and I was wrong. The verdict of the two assessors was that the two accused had committed the killing but did not intend to kill! The judge received this verdict with visible incredulity and said: 'All I have to say is that I totally disagree' and he ordered a re-trial with different assessors, as he had power to do under the law relating to criminal trials in the High Court in cases where the judge and assessors did not agree.

The retrial duly took place and the accused were found

guilty and sentenced to death, the only sentence which the judge could impose for murder.

After the retrial concluded I returned to my room in the courthouse and a police inspector came and told me that an Iban wanted to see me. I had him shown in. He was an elderly man, wearing a meagre loincloth. He addressed me in Iban and told me that he had a grievance. He was the father of one of the accused and his grievance was that he had paid a sum of money to one of the Crown witnesses to change his evidence so as to favour his son. Since the witness had not in fact changed his evidence, the father felt that he had been cheated and wanted to know if I could get his money back for him. I looked at him severely, informed him that he had committed a serious offence by bribing a witness to commit perjury. There was no possibility of me getting his money back for him and he could consider himself lucky that he was not being arrested and charged. I felt that this simple soul had suffered enough by losing his son and the money.

The police asked me if I would take the prisoners back to Kuching in my launch. Otherwise they would have to be kept under twenty-four hour guard until a police launch arrived, which would strain the very modest police manpower at Saratok. I agreed and the prisoners were brought aboard handcuffed, with an escort of two policemen, and locked in a cabin. I went to see the prisoners and sat and talked with them. I told them that they were free to appeal but that I feared that their chances of succeeding in an appeal were remote. They were apparently unconcerned. When we emerged from the river estuary into the open sea, I instructed the crew to release them from the cabin and instructed the police to remove their handcuffs. Subsequently when I visited the afterdeck, I found that the sailors had kindly provided them with cigarettes and fishing lines and they were happily sitting on the gunwhale fishing.

The Case of the
Impressionable District Officer

In my travels throughout the country, I sometimes stayed in rest houses. These were government establishments and existed only in the larger towns of which there were very few. They had a male staff, usually Malay or Iban, and provided simple accommodation and food for travelling government officers. At district headquarters lacking a rest house I stayed with the District Officer, who had to put up government visitors. These visitors were rare and the visit brief. The burden on the District Officer was not great and usually District Officers were glad to see a visitor bringing news of the outside world. There was no TV and, in my early days in Sarawak, no radio. A visit was a refreshing and interesting experience for the District Officer and, if he had one, his wife. It was also interesting for the visitor who might or might not have met them previously.

One District Officer I stayed with in a remote area asked me in a casual way after dinner if I played chess. I did. He enquired whether I would like a game. Certainly. After five or six moves I could see that I was going to lose. I am not a master player but I am not too bad. He asked if I would like to try again. I was eager to do better. We had a few more moves this time and I was more careful and more wary but this did not do me any good. I could see that I was facing a chessmaster, far above my standard, and there could be no hope for me in any game against him. Subsequently, while he was on leave in England my host committed suicide for no known reason.

I had a rather different encounter with a District Officer during a midday visit. I was on my way to a station far upriver and had stopped at a district headquarters for lunch at the invitation of the District Officer. He courteously came down to the floating jetty as I was disembarking and to my surprise he greeted me in Iban. I was more surprised on the way up to his house with him when he continued to converse in Iban. It would have seemed odd, or even rude, for me to reply in English so I felt obliged to reply in Iban. It was an Iban district but that was no reason for two government officers whose native language was English to converse in Iban. His wife did not speak Iban so when we reached the house and sat down to lunch we spoke in English.

Unfortunately this officer succumbed to the temptation, as one or two did, to identify himself with the people of his district and this affected his impartiality and his judgement. It was part of my function to receive a report on every enquiry into unnatural deaths. I received one from this officer. A party of Ibans had gone out hunting. Hunting was their greatest delight, combining the thrill of the hunt and, if successful, the reward of a feast. There was game to be had in the forests:

wild boar, deer, clouded leopard, apes, monkeys and smaller animals. Almost every adult male Iban had a shotgun. Shooting accidents were common since Ibans, in the excitement of the hunt, were inclined to shoot at any movement in the forest or undergrowth before ascertaining its cause. Iban leaders were concerned about the frequency of these accidents and wanted government to increase the penalties for culpable negligence, although this was not the answer to the problem. This particular report was typical as to the facts. A party went out one night consisting of a father, two sons, an uncle and a cousin. After they had gone some distance into the forest the father announced that for safety's sake they would split into two: one half of the party would go to the left and the other to the right. As they were separating, a wild pig ran between the two groups, and one of them promptly fired at it, missing it and killing one of the other group. The District Officer held an enquiry, as he was bound to do. It was an obvious case of manslaughter and the man should have been committed for trial in the High Court. The officer however held that for an Iban to refrain from shooting at a passing pig was to expect too much of him. Any normal Iban, according to the mindset of the officer, would have done the same thing. He characterized it simply as an unfortunate accident with no blame to be attached to anyone. I instructed the police to arrest the man responsible and charge him with manslaughter. I sent a copy of the enquiry report to the Resident, the District Officer's superior. The Resident decided that the officer concerned had been too long in an Iban area and arranged with the secretariat that he should be transferred to a distant part of the country where there were no Ibans and his Iban sympathies would be untried.

Opium Smoking in Kuching

One of the tasks I had to attend to was to give written sanction for prosecutions under the Dangerous Drugs Ordinance. A police inspector would come to see me with a file disclosing that someone was in possession of opium. For a prosecution under the Ordinance this written sanction was required and had to be produced to the magistrate or judge at the trial. Drugs were not a major problem in Sarawak at the time. The people charged were invariably elderly Chinese men at the bottom level of society working in the lowest paid labouring jobs and usually bachelors. At first I gave the sanction as a matter of course after satisfying myself that the file disclosed evidence of the possession and a chemist's report that the substance found was opium, a drug which was strictly prohibited. However after a little while I began to see things in a different light.

Exhausted after an arduous day of pedalling a trishaw around Kuching, these old men with no families would head for a room located beside Central Market where they would stretch out with a pipe of opium and relax. They were doing no harm to anyone. They were giving their tired bones a well-earned rest, relieving their aches and pains and escaping from their loneliness. The Central Police Station was nearby and whenever an eager young police inspector had nothing more pressing to do he could always go round to this room and count on finding an old man or two smoking opium. Many people in other countries have some beer or a glass of wine or spirits in the evening without harm to themselves or others, if they drink in moderation. So why then, I thought, make the lives of these old men miserable and deprive them of a harmless pleasure? In the nineteenth century, Coleridge, the justly celebrated English poet, took opium and so did the English essayist, De Quincey, and no fuss was made about that. Sherlock Holmes, one of the most famous characters in fiction, was another person who took opium and no objections were raised by the vast public who read the stories about him. So I informed the police that they need bring me no more files with proposed charges against these old men. Trafficking was different. The traffickers were gangsters who imported opium, adulterated it and made a great deal of money selling it. I prosecuted cases against traffickers personally but these cases were rare. They were usually too smart to be caught by the police. Only the little men were easily caught.

I observed from a Malayan newspaper that the wise and humane Chief Minister of Malaya, Tunku Abdul Rahman, had expressed himself on the subject of prosecuting people for opium smoking in much the same way as I was thinking. He even said that Malaya, on achieving independence, which was rapidly approaching, would substantially amend the dangerous drugs legislation to limit prosecutions. Encouraged by this I began to prepare a paper for the Government of Sarawak and the Secretary of State setting out the position and proposing changes in the law. However, this came to an abrupt end. A storm blew up in the United Nations concerning drugs when they heard Tunku Abdul Rahman's views and the U.N. strongly opposed his proposed initiative. He dropped it forthwith and I abandoned my paper although I still did not easily grant sanction for prosecutions. In those days there was no drug menace. No one took opium except the elderly and opium was the only drug taken. Heroin, cannabis, ecstasy, cocaine, amphetamines and the rest were unheard of, at least in our part of the world, and youngsters were free of this evil.

The Case of the Vain Judge

Judges used to be regarded as Olympian creatures endowed with massive erudition, remarkable intelligence, gravity, patience, the ability to see further through a brick wall than ordinary mortals, and as models of propriety. Nowadays the public are beginning to understand that judges are human like the rest of us. They may possess some of these legendary qualities in some degree. They may not. They are liable to error, as any human being is. The best of them are aware of this and the serious consequences which may ensue from their decisions when people's lives, liberty and very existence may depend on them. Humility is a great and, unfortunately, a rare virtue. It is nowhere more needed than on the judicial bench, where a man of conscience must always bear in mind that he is not omniscient or infallible and that he must consider with care whether he has arrived at the right answer and have the courage and honesty to admit that he could be wrong. It was Oliver Cromwell who, in addressing the general assembly of the Church of Scotland in 1650, said: 'I beseech you, in the bowels of Christ, think it possible that you may be wrong'. A scrutiny of his own life does not suggest that he was ever in the habit of addressing this excellent advice to himself but it is always much easier to see the error of others than to see one's own. And more difficult still to be willing to admit to what one sees or suspects of one's own fallibility.

In Britain, there was a grave miscarriage of justice in the conviction of the Guildford Four in 1975 and the Maguire Seven in 1976. They would have been sentenced to death had the death penalty not been abolished. It was not till 1989 that the conviction of the Guildford Four was quashed and only in 1991 was the Maguire Seven conviction quashed. These convictions should never have happened

In Sarawak we had a judge whose boast was that he was the youngest judge to be appointed in the colonial service. His name shall be John since that was not his name. Vanity is a regrettable characteristic but it may not always be important. In his case it was important because of his addresses to assessors in murder cases. He had to record these so that if there was an appeal, the Court of Appeal could see whether he had properly directed the assessors. He framed these addresses so as to stand up to the scrutiny of the appeal court rather than to explain the issues to the assessors in simple language, capable of being translated. The judge could speak only English. The assessors were unsophisticated village people who knew no English. The interpreters could speak English and the local language required in the case, usually the lingua franca, Malay but Iban was also common. There were many other languages in Sarawak. The education of the interpreters was modest and the refinement of legal language was beyond them, as indeed it is beyond most native English speakers. This judge had a still more serious defect. He suffered from a sense of racial superiority that was noticeable in his attitude in court to parties and witnesses.

In a longhouse in the far interior of Sarawak there lived a community who had come over the mountain barrier between Sarawak and Kalimantan or Indonesian Borneo. They spoke their own language, Lahanan. They worked their hill farms and had little contact with any other longhouses which were much further downriver. They lived simple, self-sufficient lives. One night an unseemly quarrel sprang up. A young husband and his wife were seated crosslegged on the bamboo floor of the public part of the longhouse. The wife was vehemently criticizing her husband. In the hearing of others she accused him of being sexually inadequate and failing to satisfy her. She became shrill and malicious and, irritated by his silence and apparent calmness, she leaned towards him and tore the necklace from his neck. Peoples of the interior of both sexes commonly wore necklaces, bangles at their wrists and knees and earrings of leopard's teeth or decorative artefacts. The necklaces were colourful and often made of beads of considerable antiquity, highly valued by the community. They were naturally a source of pride to the fortunate owners, whose possessions were few and simple. The action of the wife in snatching the necklace from her young husband's neck and breaking it in the process was, and was clearly intended to be, the most grievous of insults. The husband was deeply shocked. He took up his parang, the long all-purpose heavy machete, which all men carried for working purposes, and struck her mortally.

He then went down with other inhabitants of the longhouse to the nearest district office and reported the matter to the police. He did not attempt to excuse himself. The police investigation file duly arrived on my desk. I framed a charge of murder. There was no doubt that he had intentionally killed her and there could be no other charge. In due course I travelled by longboat far upriver to the district headquarters for the trial. The judge in the case was John. The accused was undefended. The assessors were headmen from longhouses in the area. They were bare-bodied but splendidly attired in flowered loincloths, with beautifully made rotan hats adorned with great black and white hornbill plumes, the teeth of clouded leopards piercing their ear lobes, their necklaces and bangles colourful and exquisite.

The judge took his seat on the bench with, as was his wont, no greeting to them or any sign of recognition. Language was a problem. Since the judge spoke no language but English I was obliged to conduct the Crown case in English. The accused and the witnesses spoke Lahanan. The assessors understood simple Malay, although this was not their language. We thus had to have an interpreter who spoke Malay and Lahanan. The District Officer had produced someone who was alleged to speak these two languages. I don't know how good his Lahanan was but his Malay was not impressive. We also had to have another interpreter to translate from Malay into English for the benefit of the judge who would otherwise not have understood a word of the proceedings. He also had to translate from English, spoken by the judge and perforce by me, to Malay. This interpreter was Malay but he had to adapt his Malay to the understanding of the Lahanan–Malay interpreter, as became obvious in the course of the proceedings. His English was satisfactory if the vocabulary was limited and the syntax kept simple. So everything that was said had to go through two interpreters neither of whom was familiar with the language of the law or the concepts of the law. It was not the ideal way of ensuring perfect understanding. However it is an imperfect world and the administration of justice, as everyone who has to do with it knows, shares in the imperfection.

The witnesses testified to what had happened on the lines set out above. The accused young man offered no defence. He sat in the dock with his head cast down, in evident great sadness.

It then fell to me to address the assessors.

I recounted the undisputed facts. It was quite clear that the accused had killed his wife and the blow was such that he must have known that it was likely to cause her death. On the face of it that was murder but it was necessary to consider the circumstances. Was he provoked? This in certain circumstances could reduce the gravity of the offence to culpable homicide not amounting to murder. At this point the judge intervened. He said that I was counsel for the Crown and not for the defence and said that I should confine myself to the Crown case. I pointed out in reply that the accused person was unrepresented by counsel. He had no one to speak for him, that my duty was to see that the case was presented fairly by the Crown and it would not be presented fairly if the assessors were not made aware of the law on provocation. The judge then grew heated. He said that he and not I was in charge of the court and that he would decide on what could be said and what could not. I said that I spoke for the Crown and had a duty to see that justice was done. I asked him if he was ordering me to discontinue my address. If so, I would comply but I would wish his order to be placed on record since this issue could go further. He backed down and avoided the question by telling me to confine myself to what was relevant. Since the issue of provocation was highly relevant and a man's life was at stake, I continued my address, explained to the assessors that the gravity of the offence would be reduced if there was provocation. The provocation must be both grave and sudden. If that was proved, the offence would not be murder but the lesser offence of culpable homicide. Obviously there was provocation and the evidence showed that it was sudden. What they had to consider and what I emphasized, to the annoyance of the judge, was that they, being members of a community similar to that of the accused and familiar with its culture, were in the best position to say whether the provocation was of sufficient gravity to merit reducing the offence. I concluded my address by stating that my presentation was subject to anything that the judge might say in his summing up since they were bound to follow any directions given by him.

The judge then began his address to the assessors. There were references to cases decided in the Court of King's Bench in

London, complete with reference to the years and the volumes of the law reports and the page numbers of the reports. It was obvious to me that he had prepared all this before leaving his chambers in Kuching. I had a mental picture of the assessors, in all their finery, returning to their remote longhouses, entering their library and selecting from the shelves the appropriate volumes of the King's Bench reports for considered perusal. The Malay interpreter had, of course to translate this learned discourse to the assessors. The law references were gibberish to him and he simply omitted them from his translation. Although he did not understand a word of Malay, the judge could not but know this but he was concerned about having on record a learned address to impress the Court of Appeal with his erudition. The way he recounted the evidence and the way he referred to my address on provocation was unfavourable to the accused. Verbal emphasis and body language are potent means of communication, particularly when the words themselves which are being used are not understood by the hearers and are being crudely translated. The assessors returned a verdict of murder as the judge evidently wanted them to do. He then proceeded to pronounce the death sentence with no trace of humanity or even courtesy.

However the man was not hanged. Every death sentence had to be reviewed by the Governor in Council. They had my written report before them and the Governor exercised the Royal Prerogative and commuted the sentence to imprisonment for life. This would be regularly reviewed and would almost certainly result in the release of the man before too long.

I spoke privately to the Attorney General about the manner in which the judge conducted this trial and his other trials and about his objection to my conduct of the Crown case. I have no doubt the Governor was informed of this. He had his ear close to the ground and had many sources of information. At the end of his first tour of duty the judge went on leave and did not return. He was not missed.

The Case of the Iban Killer who did not Commit Murder

Murder means killing with the intention of killing and with none of the factors that can reduce culpability. Amongst these factors is mental disorder, which causes persons not to be responsible for their actions. An example of this can be seen in the trial of a young Iban who had been sitting talking early one morning with his elder brother and the elder brother's wife. The elder brother departed to go to his farm. A short time later the younger brother ran up to him to tell him that he had just killed his wife. There was no trace of animosity in the history of the case or of any other reason for the killing. The judge rightly found him guilty of the killing and ordered that he be detained during the pleasure of the Governor. On the evening after the trial I went to see the young man in his cell. I asked him if he could tell me any more about how the event happened. He spoke very gently and softly. He said he saw a red cloud in front of his eyes. He was not aware of the act of killing and was horrified when he saw what had happened.

A similar incident occurred in Kuching. A man went into

a hardware shop where there were several customers. He stood idly among them for a few minutes. Then he picked up a machete which was amongst the articles for sale and hacked off the arm of a waiting customer, a man totally unknown to him. He was duly charged with inflicting grievous hurt before the senior magistrate. He could give no explanation for his act. The magistrate was compassionate and was unwilling to order him to be detained during the Governor's pleasure, which could mean being detained for life in the mental asylum. Instead he sentenced him to a term of imprisonment. The prison rules did not permit solitary confinement except as a punishment for serious disobedience to the prison rules. Accordingly this man was in a cell with two other prisoners. In the middle of the night he seized the latrine bucket and dashed out the brains of one of his fellow prisoners.

Such people are sadly afflicted. Unfortunately there is no telling what they will do and do without warning. They have to be detained and this can be for life, since there are cases on record of people under such detention who behave well for years in prison and then, being released, kill again.

Attorney Generalship and New Responsibilities

The Attorney General was my superior, the principal law officer of the Crown, a member of the Supreme Council and the second man in the government after the Chief Secretary. He was very senior in the colonial service. He had a powerful intellect, was very able and had no time for fools. He was ebullient and masterful. Apart from his work, which he invariably tackled with relish, his interests were bridge and golf. He and his wife, Jo, who was very much a grande dame of considerable wealth, were brilliant bridge players of international standard. We had a judge with a phenomenal memory. He could read a page of a book, close it and recite the whole page with no error. George, Jo, the judge and I played bridge every Saturday night when the judge and I were not away from Kuching.

At the end of my first year in Sarawak, George had, I knew, to make a confidential report on me, which was sent to the Governor and the Secretary of State for the colonies in London. I was not informed of the contents of the report but, under general orders, George had to inform me of any criticism he made of me in it. George called me into his chambers and informed me that he had a criticism to make. He was reporting to the Secretary of State that I was too friendly to the local people. I was astonished to learn that this was a fault and told him so. He said I did not mix much with fellow officers in the government. I pointed out that we played bridge every week that I was in Kuching, I never refused an invitation to dine with other colonial officers and I frequently entertained them to dinner in my house. Certainly I also entertained Malays, Chinese, Ibans, Kayans, Kenyahs and other local people. When I was travelling I was entertained by them in their villages or longhouses in the interior and they were unstinting in their modest hospitality. When they visited Kuching they came to see me and they were welcome to stay or have a meal. I did not see that extending to them the friendship and hospitality that I extended to my fellow colonial officers was incompatible with my official status or function. I could not promise to change in this. Well, said George, who did not easily change his mind either, 'I have told you as I am bound to do. Perhaps the Secretary of State will view this differently.'

A few years passed and I heard no more of criticism in my annual reports. Then came one weekend when George, who had obtained a government launch for the weekend, invited me to join him, his wife and their 17-year-old son, who was in Sarawak on holiday, on a visit to an island. The island was uninhabited but was well known as a place where turtles came to lay their eggs. We departed on Saturday afternoon and by nightfall were anchored off the small island. We had dinner on deck under the stars. A sailor rowed us ashore in the launch's dinghy. We remained ashore for some time and watched in the starlight the great heavy creatures slowly and laboriously make their way from the water's edge up the sloping sandy shore, excavate a deep hole with their rear flippers and deposit a hundred or more eggs in them. They then filled in the hole and began to make their ponderous way back to the sea and swim into the deep and the night. The effort they had to make was considerable and they appeared to be weeping over it. In fact their tears which, were copious, are a way of keeping sand out of their eyes.

I had noticed that George was unusually sombre and thoughtful during the voyage back. We arrived in Kuching on Sunday evening and on Monday morning he called me into his chambers and informed me that he was leaving on the midday plane for Singapore and then on to London. He told me that he had recommended to the Governor that I should be appointed in his place and the Governor had approved. Subject to the approval of the Secretary of State this would be gazetted. This came as a surprise and characteristically George offered no explanation. Only after he had gone and I had taken his place, the Director of Medical Services informed me that George had stomach cancer at an advanced stage and he was not expected to return. He did not return. I missed him very much as my superior and as a friend.

George left a mass of Bills that he had been preparing for the next legislative session of Council Negri, the legislature of Sarawak. My first task was to write explanatory notes for each of these to be attached to the Bills when they were printed and gazetted. I would then have to move the Bills at the session of Council Negri and deal with any questions or objections or proposed amendments. By far the most important of the Bills was a new Land Code.

Sarawak's land laws were contained in a tangle of legislation. We had commissioned the services of an expert from New Zealand, which had basically the same system of registered title as Sarawak, to advise us on the drafting of a comprehensive Land Code. George had taken exclusive charge of this project and worked with the Director of Lands and Surveys and the expert. I had had no knowledge of what was being done. I now studied the Land Code Bill which had been prepared. The drafting of this had been completed and George had set up a Select Committee of the Council Negri comprising leading Malays, Ibans and Chinese who had approved it. Unfortunately I found what seemed to me to be a few flaws in it. I asked the Director of Lands and Surveys to come and see me. He was a very senior man. He came and said to me: 'Up to now you have been under the Attorney General. The ultimate responsibility for all your work was his and you could refer difficulties to him. The final decisions now rest with you. Now the weight of responsibility is entirely on your shoulders and I know you will be feeling it.' He was absolutely right and I was grateful for his understanding and his help. I re-convened the Select Committee and explained the provisions of the Bill which I thought were flawed and how I thought the flaws could be rectified. They left the matters entirely to me. The Bill was very lengthy and complicated and I could not blame them for pushing the entire responsibility back to me.

There was one matter, however, which found no place in the proposed new code. Under the law all land was divided into zones. The vast area of the interior was one of these zones and there was no provision for a registered title within it. The people of the interior, the majority of the population, were, as they had been for centuries, farmers growing rice, their staple diet. Although their lands had never been surveyed or demarcated in any way they all knew what land belonged to them—in the sense that it was theirs to cultivate as it had been their forefathers'. It was the very foundation of their lives. I was concerned that they had no legal rights to the land, only customary rights and these were not embodied in or recognized by the proposed new comprehensive Land Code, as they were not in the existing law. They never had been. In a society which had been politically and economically static for many generations, land titles in the interior had not been an issue. But times were changing rapidly. Timber was valuable and the interior was heavily forested with primary forest over thirty million years old containing magnificent trees over a hundred feet high. Sawmills were being developed and timber companies were being granted concessions. These trees were particularly valuable. It was not difficult to foresee that concessions could be granted which would encroach on the customary rights of people who lived and farmed areas over the areas conceded; people could lose their homes as well as the source of their livelihood. The government's duty was to serve the people and protect their rights. This was one of the principles of the Brookes and was surely our duty too. Admittedly the question of how to legislate for this protection was a difficult one and once the question was raised, it was bound to raise controversy. Many interests were involved and whatever solution was arrived at by the government would be unpopular and opposed by some of these interested parties.

No consideration had been given to the matter by our New Zealand adviser or by the department of lands or by the Select Committee. This was not their responsibility. It was a major policy issue and could only be brought up at the highest level. The question facing me, as the officer on behalf of the government responsible for the proposed new code and with the duty of presenting and explaining it to the Council Negri for them to vote on, was how could we proceed to promulgate a new Land Code which was intended to be, and purported to be, comprehensive without addressing this issue? I resolved to raise the question with the Chief Secretary, who functioned as Speaker of the Council, and had lengthy discussions with him. There was no simple answer. The Chief Secretary was new to Sarawak and had come from another colony. He had little knowledge of the country or its peoples or their way of life. Whatever measures the government proposed would raise an outcry, including an outcry from some amongst the people we were aiming to protect. We both knew that the colonial era of Sarawak was drawing to a close and in a few years the country would be independent. The Chief Secretary's view was that we should leave the matter to be dealt with by the government elected after independence and we would avoid the odium and civil trouble which legislation by us would inevitably involve. I felt that we should spare no effort in solving the matter, impossible though it would be to please everyone. If we were unpopular, so be it, we were departing anyway. It would be much more difficult for an elected government to deal with this. Members of the elected government would have a personal interest which would influence their judgement. We had no such interest. Our sole concern was the protection of the rights of the people of the interior. An elected government must please the majority and would be reluctant to put forward legislation that would arouse controversy. The Chief Secretary was concerned about the effect on the colonial office in London if there was civil commotion. Our primary responsibility was to maintain peace and order. We would be held responsible for civil disorder. That was the view expressed by the Chief Secretary. To me what mattered was doing the best we could for the vulnerable people of the interior and not the approval of a minister in another government, almost seven thousand miles away. I thought that we should grasp the nettle. However the Chief Secretary would not agree and without his co-operation I could take the matter no further. He had, of course, a point. His part in the peaceful and orderly administration of Sarawak was recognized by the colonial office in his subsequent appointment as Governor of another territory.

The sitting of the Council Negri began. Members came from all over the country. There were three official government members, the three principal officers of government: the Chief Secretary, the Attorney General and the Financial Secretary. The Chief Secretary was the Speaker. Although by far the youngest and most junior of the three, I was, by virtue of my office, the leader on the government side. Also by virtue of my office I had to present an unprecedented number of Bills, explain why the government thought them necessary and move the resolutions to pass them. I had to do a great deal of homework and burn much midnight oil familiarizing myself with all the provisions in the Bills so as to be able to answer any questions that the members might put. The nightmare was the new Land Code Bill. It was very long and contained very many detailed provisions. It was also by far the most important piece of legislation that had been put to the Council Negri. It affected everyone and I had to anticipate a host of questions. The government was apprehensive about it and the Governor and the Chief Secretary were probably wondering how this junior person in the role of Attorney General would be able to cope. I was wondering the same myself. It was a baptism of fire.

The moment of truth came and I rose to address the Council Negri for the first time. I knew many of the members. Malay was the lingua franca and was spoken by all the members except the Chief Secretary—the new man who replaced the former Chief Secretary—and the Financial Secretary. They were the only two Europeans in the Council apart from myself. The Chief Secretary was in the chair as Speaker. I decided to speak in Malay and not in English. This had not been done before from the government side. There were interpreters to interpret English speeches for non-English speakers and conversely but I wanted to be able to speak directly to members. I did not anticipate much difficulty with the Bills except for the Land Code. I addressed the Council on them and moved them one by one. The Financial Secretary formally seconded the motions and they all passed without difficulty. Then I came to the Land Code Bill. I delivered my address on this, outlined its principal provisions and explained the necessity for them as clearly and cogently as I could. I moved that the Bill be passed and sat down with trepidation, expecting a torrent of questions and detailed objections to which I would be expected to have an answer. The Financial Secretary formally seconded my proposal and sat down. We waited in silence. After a few minutes, the Speaker said that since there appeared to be no questions or objections, he presumed that the Bill could now be taken to be passed unanimously. No one challenged this presumption and the Bill became law subject to the consent of the Governor, which could be taken for granted.

But one Bill was objected to. It was a very short, simple Bill designed to put a stop to people collecting wild orchids from our abundant primary forest without a licence. A number of members took strong exception to this. I had not thought there were so many ardent orchid fanciers amongst members. I informed the Council that since a number of members were unhappy with the Bill I would withdraw the motion to pass it and the government would reconsider its necessity.

The experience was a striking illustration of how business

is done not only in legislative assemblies but on many boards and committees. Major complicated matters are dealt with in a very short time because many members do not understand the issues or have not taken the trouble to study them. They keep quiet. But when the item of the agenda is something very simple, everyone has an opinion. Professor Parkinson in his entertaining treatise on Parkinson's Law says that a board of directors contemplating a project costing many millions will approve it in a matter of minutes. The next item on the agenda is where the office boy parks his bicycle and two hours is spent arguing on this. Exaggerated of course. Parkinson seeks to be amusing. But it contains more than a grain of truth.

The Case of Murder and Gold

There was only one murder case in which I prosecuted a woman and it happened that the victim was also a woman. The victim was the elderly wife of a retired customs officer in Sibu. She supplemented her husband's modest pension by selling gold articles of jewellery, cycling round the houses, visiting housewives in their homes. Gold jewellery was regarded as a form of savings and if a housewife had some money to spare she would invest it in gold bangles or rings or chains or brooches. This lady carried round a selection of these to display to potential customers.

On the outskirts of the town there was an isolated house with the name, ominous as it happened, of Journey's End. The house was a simple wooden house, raised on piles as were most houses, with wooden shutters in place of glass windows. The house was rented by an English assistant of one of the commercial houses which imported and exported goods. This young man had taken a Malay mistress, aged 21, who lived with him in the house, as did her brother. The Englishman was normally out all day at his office in town while the mistress kept house and her brother, who did not encumber himself with a fixed occupation, came and went and sometimes invited over his friends.

The elderly lady came round one day on her bicycle and stopped at the house. She knew well enough who lived there. There were few secrets in the small towns of Sarawak. Everyone knew everyone else and few movements escaped observation. The lady called out from the foot of the stairs leading up to the door, as was the polite custom. The shutters were open, as they normally were during the day for ventilation. The young mistress looked out and invited the lady to come up. This she did and they sat down to chat. The selection of jewellery was produced, examined, discussed and admired. The mistress had no money. She relied, of course, on her lover for support. She explained to the lady that she would want to buy several articles but needed a few days to get the money ready. She asked the lady to return a week later and to bring with her the full selection of her jewellery so that the mistress could make a choice. The lady went happily away, thinking of the profitable business she would soon be doing. The mistress promptly began to discuss with her brother, a friend of his and a young prostitute of the town, who was also a friend and who happened to be visiting, what they would do when the lady returned. One of the things they did before the return visit was to dig a grave behind the house.

The lady returned the following week. She was invited to enter the house, little knowing what fate awaited her. They all sat on the floor as was the custom and the lady brought out her collection of gold personal ornaments. While she was doing this, the brother came up behind her with a large lump of charcoal in his hand and struck her on the back of the head with it. He struck her several times. They put a gag in her mouth to stifle her cries and bound her hands and feet with wire. They then deposited her, still alive, in the grave and covered her with earth. There was a considerable amount of blood in the room where the murder took place.

It happened to be the day of the week when a boy came to cut the grass. The boy noticed the lady's bicycle parked near the stairs and that the house, contrary to custom, was all shut up, door and window shutters closed. He called out. After a few moments a shutter was partly opened and the mistress looked out. She was not wearing a blouse and had only a brassiere on the upper half of her body, which was all that was visible. She bade the boy go away in peremptory tones and closed the shutter again. The boy turned away thinking the situation very odd. At this point he noticed what looked like blood seeping through the cracks in the plank floor onto the ground below. He mounted his bicycle and quickly pedalled to the office of the English commercial assistant who had employed him to cut the grass. He related to him what he had seen. The Englishman got into his car to drive to the house but, as luck would have it, his car broke down and he was considerably delayed in arriving. When he finally arrived he saw that the floor had been recently washed but that there were still spots of what looked like blood on the walls and ledges. He enquired what had happened and his mistress told him that she had had a miscarriage. This satisfied him and he questioned her no further. That night, as they were about to go to sleep, she asked him to close the shutters. They always left the shutters open for some fresh air. Why, he asked, did she want them closed. If left open, she said, ghosts could enter. This objection had not been made before but he did not pursue the matter. He was unaware that right outside the window was a fresh grave.

The old lady's disappearance did not, of course, go unremarked. Her family were concerned when she did not return home. They knew of her gold trade but robbery was almost unknown in those days. Muggings were unheard of. People went about their affairs in perfect safety day and night. Doors were frequently left unlocked and shutters left open. However the family knew that she had gone out with a valuable gold collection and her non-return was ominous. The police were informed. The amateurish mode of the murder made discovery a simple matter. The new grave was found and the body disinterred. A search uncovered the hoard of gold ornaments concealed in a tree near the house. The boy was interviewed. The Englishman was interviewed. From his report to the police it appeared that he was more concerned that the scandal and the publicity of a murder trial could gravely prejudice his employment situation than he was about the fate of the old lady. The police also found out that there had been four people in the house and their identity.

The difficulty in the case was that only those four people knew and could tell us what had actually happened in the house. We had evidence that the old lady was murdered for her jewellery and that the murder had taken place in the house, but who committed the murder? The police had statements from all four who were present and we knew very well what had happened but the statements were not admissible in evidence. We needed a witness.

I framed charges of murder against all four, the mistress, her brother, the prostitute and the young male friend. Apart from the information set out above, we had the evidence of the technical assistant of the government pathology laboratory that the blood stains in the house were of the same group as the old lady. The Chief of Police had personally led the investigation and had taken scrapings of the blood stains, sealed them in envelopes and sent them to the laboratory in Kuching. Further, the brother had had a physical examination by a government doctor who had observed curious puncture wounds on the thumbs of both his hands. He was discussing this with a dentist colleague who promptly said: 'I know what those are!' He had had occasion to examine the mouth of a young patient who strongly resisted examination and he had to forcibly open the patient's mouth with his two hands, using his thumbs to force the jaws apart. The patient bit his thumbs with his incisors making precisely the wounds seen on the brother's thumbs. It therefore seemed that the brother had forced the gag into the victim's mouth and suffered what the dentist suffered in consequence. This was strong evidence of the brother's implication in the murder but what about his sister? We knew from the statements that she was the principal but had no evidence to put before the court.

By this time there was a daily air service in elderly DC3s between Kuching and Sibu. I flew to Sibu the day before the trial and found myself seated in the plane beside the laboratory technical assistant whom I had called to testify to the blood group of the samples. Having more than a passing interest in forensic medicine, sometimes called medical jurisprudence and one of the subjects covered in my law degree, I knew something of the different methods of typing blood and would have liked to discuss these with the assistant but he seemed curiously reserved and uncommunicative so I did not pursue the discussion.

When travelling on duty and staying at a district headquarters I could stay in the government rest house or, if the District Officer or Chief of Police was a friend, I might be invited to stay with them. In this case the police chief was a friend and I accepted his invitation, the more readily in that it gave me a better opportunity to discuss the details of the case with the man who had led the very thorough investigation. I was having a bath on the evening of my arrival when the chief informed me through the bathroom door that the lover of the principal accused had arrived and wanted to see me. I asked the chief to find out what he wanted to say. He had come, he said, to ask me to keep the name of his company out of the proceedings. I asked the chief to inform him that my function was to present all facts relevant to the murder to the court. Whether the identity of his company would emerge I could not predict but it was no part of my function to conceal this or prevent it emerging. In fact during the trial the young gardener, when describing how he had mounted his bicycle and rushed off to see his employer at his office, did mention the name of the company.

I asked the chief to get one of his inspectors to interview the prostitute who, like the others, was in custody, and tell her that if she would agree to testify to the commission of the murder, as she had done in her statement, I would withdraw the charge against her. The fourth accused, the young man, had taken no active part in the affair and was a passive and somewhat unwilling observer. I had the police make the same proposal to him. Without actual witness testimony the prosecution would fail, certainly against the principal accused, if not also against her brother who was an active accomplice.

The next day the trial began in the High Court. The court was packed with every member of the public able to get in and there was still a crowd outside. The crime was sensational. The old lady was known to everyone in the small town and related to many. I usually prosecuted in Malay or Iban, depending on the language spoken by those involved, since this avoided the delays and misunderstandings caused by using interpreters. However, the judge at this trial only spoke English so I spoke in English and an interpreter interpreted everything into Malay for the benefit of the accused and witnesses. All of them were Malay except the prostitute who was Iban but she was fluent in Malay.

I informed the court that I was withdrawing the charges against two of the accused. I also informed the court that they had been invited to give evidence for the Crown on the understanding that the charges against them would be withdrawn. The court would no doubt bear that in mind since the withdrawal of the charge was a considerable inducement and it was for the court to decide whether and to what extent this might affect the veracity of their evidence.

A member of the family of the victim told the court of the lady's trading activities. She had gone out on the fateful day with all her gold articles. No, she did not say where she was going. She frequently went out and visited various houses where she thought there were possibilities of a sale. She was gone all day, which was a little unusual. They did not worry until night fell and she had not returned. Their concern grew as the night advanced and still she did not return. They went out to various houses of relatives and friends but none had news of her. Finally they went to the police.

A police inspector gave evidence of the report of the family and the investigations which he instituted. These led to the house known as Journey's End. A search of the surroundings revealed the disturbed earth and the new grave and its gruesome contents. A further search discovered the gold ornaments. The gardener gave his evidence of the strange goings-on when he went to the house. He was followed by the English assistant who was, as he might well be, very uncomfortable in the witness box. Since he had been told by the principal accused that she had had a miscarriage, I called, as a witness, a doctor who had been asked to examine her. He stated that there was no evidence of any miscarriage.

The next witness was the laboratory assistant. He testified

to having received envelopes from the police. I showed him the envelopes and he identified them, having in fact signed them. He confirmed that the contents were dried blood and identified the group as being that of the sample of the victim's blood also sent to him. Having obtained this evidence from him, I sat down and was casually looking at the envelopes of the blood samples while this witness was being cross-examined by defence counsel. With a shock it dawned on me that the sealed envelopes showed no mark of ever having been opened. I rose immediately and asked the judge to adjourn the hearing. This he did and I went straight to the Chief of Police's office with the envelope, which we both scrutinized. The chief confirmed that they were exactly as sealed by him and there was no trace of them ever having been opened. I recalled that on the plane the laboratory assistant had been singularly unwilling to answer my questions about which test he used and did not want to discuss the matter. I asked the chief to have one of his inspectors show the envelopes to the laboratory assistant and put it to him that they had never been opened and there never was any test. The inspector came back to us and said that the witness had with great reluctance been compelled to admit that this was the case. His excuse was that he was busy! I went back to the court and asked the judge and the assessors to disregard entirely the evidence given by this witness.

The prostitute then gave evidence. This was a crucial witness and I had to hope that she would stick to her undertaking to relate all that had happened. The charge against her had already been withdrawn and if she prevaricated there was little

I could do. She was clearly unhappy in the witness box and did not want to speak of what she had seen. She squirmed and tried to evade giving any except vague answers to questions. Patience and, more important, persistence eventually got the whole sordid story out of her. The young man gave evidence. He was very unhappy too but his story bore out what the prostitute said. That concluded the case for the Crown.

Defence counsel then made a bold effort to have the case dismissed without the defence being called on. He pointed out that the seeping red liquid which the boy saw was not proved to be blood. He avoided all mention of the alleged miscarriage. The European and the police had observed marks of what appeared to be blood and the police had taken scrapings. But were they blood? The Crown had asked the court to disregard the laboratory evidence. There was then no evidence that what had been seen was in fact blood. As for the evidence given by the prostitute and the young man, people will say anything to save their own skin. Well, he did his best for his clients but the judge was unimpressed and ruled that the Crown had established a *prima facie* case which called for an answer.

There was a noticeable frisson amongst the public as the principal accused took her seat in the witness box. She had a bold look and, as it turned out, she was pert in her answers. She was well turned out and was wearing make-up but I noticed that her finger nails were cut very short which seemed out of keeping. I wondered if blood had coagulated underneath her nails and she had cut them short in order to remove all traces. I decided to begin with some questions about this.

'You look after your appearance rather well, do you not?'

To my astonishment the interpreter translated my question into Malay as: 'You look after Europeans rather well?'! This caused an even greater frisson in court as the public thought they were now going to hear some interesting and scandalous details about her relationship with the Englishman. I hastily corrected the interpreter, to the disappointment of the public.

Her reply was: 'You look after your appearance rather well too.' Presumably she was referring to my dress in wig and gown. I abandoned the line of questioning and began to put the main points of the Crown case to her.

The old lady had come to her house a week before she came by her death? Yes.

She had brought gold ornaments? Yes.

The accused asked her to come back and bring all her ornaments? No, she didn't.

She in fact came back? I never saw her.

Why did she send away the young gardener who came to cut the grass? The grass didn't need cutting.

But it was his regular day for cutting the grass? The grass didn't need cutting that day.

Had she ever sent him away before? She couldn't remember.

Could she explain how it was that he saw what looked like blood dripping from between the floorboards? She had no idea about that.

She had told her paramour that she had had a miscarriage? She didn't remember telling him that.

In fact she did not have a miscarriage? No answer.

Why did she ask him to close the shutters that night? She did not remember telling him that.

The old lady had been brutally killed by repeated blows with a heavy object and buried behind the house. Had she any explanation for this? She knew nothing about that.

The gold ornaments were found hidden in a nearby tree? She didn't know that.

Her girlfriend and the young man had said that she had planned the killing of the old lady and had carried it out with her brother. What had she to say about that? It wasn't true.

Why would they tell lies about such a serious matter? They know, I don't.

And so it went on. There was nothing she could say to rebut the Crown case. Her brother was unable to do any better.

Defence counsel addressed the court and said more or less what he had said earlier when asking for the Crown case to be dismissed. In view of the performance of his clients in the witness box it was less convincing than it was the first time. I then addressed the Court. Even without the two key witnesses, the Crown had proved beyond a peradventure that the old lady was murdered in Journey's End and that the principal accused was in the house at the time and her dress and behaviour indicated that something unusual was happening. The old lady's injuries indicated serious loss of blood and there was evidence of what appeared to be bloodstains in the house. The accused had lied to her paramour about this. Why? And why was she fearful of ghosts that night when she had no fear on previous nights? The body and the ornaments were secreted nearby. The only question that the court need address was: Who was the killer? For the answer to that we had to look to the testimony of the two people who were present at the planning and the killing and who told us that the deed was planned by the two accused and carried out by them. Neither of these two witnesses admitted any active participation and the court might wonder whether they were being strictly truthful about their part. However their conduct, whatever it might be, was not the subject of the trial. What was in issue was simply whether the two accused were guilty of the murder. The two witnesses had originally been charged with participation in the murder and had bought their freedom by agreeing to give evidence for the Crown. This was something to be taken into account in assessing their credibility. The house was not theirs: they were mere visitors. There was no evidence to suggest that they had taken a leading part in the murder. The two accused had not sought to put the blame for the murder on them. Of the four people in the house, one or more were responsible for the murder. Was the Court satisfied beyond reasonable doubt on all the evidence that the two accused were responsible? If not, it was their duty to acquit. The Crown's contention was that the responsibility was proved beyond reasonable doubt.

The judge summed up to the assessors. He went over the evidence. The onus of proof was on the Crown: it was not for the accused to prove their innocence. There could be no doubt that the old lady was murdered and murdered in the house. Was the murder committed by either of the two accused or by both? There was no evidence to suggest that one could be guilty but not the other. The two eyewitnesses testified that both the accused had murdered the old lady. If their evidence was believed the verdict on both the accused must be guilty. If the assessors had any reasonable doubt about the veracity of their evidence on this point, they must find them not guilty. The assessors then were invited to retire and discuss their verdict. They soon returned. Their finding was guilty. The judge solemnly pronounced the death sentence and that was that.

Both the accused travelled to Kuching where the central prison containing the execution chamber was situated. I was informed that a huge crowd turned up to see the principal accused and her brother taken aboard the ship that plied this route and that when she walked up the gangway onto the deck the young woman turned around to look at the crowd, put her hand to her neck and jerked her head back with an air of defiance. Both of them appealed but the appeal was hopeless. I did not see her in the Court of Appeal since she was seated behind me but I was told that she was looking wretched.

All sentences of death came automatically for review before the Governor in Council. The Supreme Council consisted of the Chief Secretary, the Attorney General and the Financial Secretary and the unofficial members, being respectively leaders of the Malay community, the Iban community and the Chinese community. The Governor presided since the prerogative of mercy was his and the other members of the Council were his advisers. It was my duty in capital cases to submit a report for consideration by the Council. I prepared this, setting out the facts of the case, drawing attention to the cold-blooded planning and the brutality. I also pointed out the fact that this was the first death penalty case involving a woman.

The Chief Secretary was the best type of fair-minded, uncomplicated, straightforward Englishman. He had been a District Officer under the Third Rajah, knew Sarawak and its people as well as anyone and was their very faithful servant. He came to my chambers to see me the afternoon before the Council meeting and asked me whether I thought the penalty on the woman should be carried out or commuted to life imprisonment. I told him that there were no mitigating factors in the case which was the worst case of murder we had ever had. The only question was whether a woman should be treated differently from a man. There could be no rational basis for making a distinction. That was enough for the Chief Secretary who went off with his mind clear on his decision.

At this time, the Attorney General, my respected colleague and friend and brilliant bridge partner had departed from Sarawak. He had been diagnosed as suffering from cancer, which was found to be at a terminal stage. The Secretary of State, on the recommendation of the Governor, had appointed me in his place. I was therefore a member of the Supreme Council and the Governor would want my advice on whether the sentence should be carried out. I spent a sleepless night mulling over the issue. I had prosecuted many capital cases but the verdict and sentence were not my responsibility. Now I had to face up to the question whether I agreed with the principle of the death penalty and whether it should be applied in this case. I had no difficulty with the second part of the question. My difficulty was with the principle. Parliament in Britain had earlier abolished the death penalty and we had had a communication from the Secretary of State recommending its abolition in Sarawak. I had consulted the various community leaders on this and they had unanimously and strongly rejected the recommendation. So the penalty was still the only penalty provided by law for murder. After a restless night I went off the next day to the meeting. I had still not arrived at a decision. The Governor asked me to open the subject and I gave the Council an account of the murder and of the proceedings. Since I had personally arranged and conducted the prosecution I informed the Governor that I would prefer that he ask the other members of the Council for their opinion before I expressed mine since I did not wish my opinion to influence them. The Governor went round each member. They were all quite definite that the sentence should be carried out. Then he came to me. At this point I found that I could not in conscience vote for the death penalty and stated this. The Governor thanked us all and ruled that the sentence should stand.

There was the laboratory assistant to be dealt with. I had him charged with perjury and committed for trial in the High Court. The Director of Medical Services, the head of his department telephoned me and protested. The man had a heavy workload and had not been able to do the tests. Would I not withdraw the charge? I was astonished. Neither the Director nor the assistant knew the facts of the case. They did know however that it was a murder case. For all they knew the evidence given by the assistant could have made the difference between a conviction or an acquittal, a matter of life or death to an accused person. Having a heavy workload was no excuse for coming to court and giving false evidence that he had examined the substance sent to him, that it was blood and blood of certain type when in fact he had not even opened the envelopes. The charge would proceed.

Some years later I was in Kuala Lumpur and was invited by American friends to the wedding of their very charming daughter. I attended the wedding ceremony in the church and when the bride and groom turned away from the altar and processed up the nave to the entrance I observed with surprise that the groom was the young man who had been the paramour of the murderess. I wondered if the bride or her parents knew of his history. Somehow I think they did not. It was not for me to tell them about it at this stage. It would be charitable to assume that he was a reformed character.

Leave and a Perilous
Syrian Encounter

On my first leave, after two and a half years, I decided to
travel back to Europe, not by a passenger liner sailing
directly from Singapore but by a freighter. I obtained a passage
on the *New York Maru*, a Japanese cargo ship of the Nippon
Yusen Kaisha line, the biggest shipping line in the world. It was
bound for Istanbul but would be calling in at ports en route to
load or unload cargo.

I travelled to Singapore by ship from Kuching and went to
the dock area of the Singapore port. There I found the *New
York Maru* looming high and vast over a jetty. I boarded it
in the evening as we were due to sail in the early morning. I
walked up the gangway. There was no one about. I walked
along a corridor and saw through an open door a man in
underclothes reading a newspaper. He looked up at me and
then hastily resumed his reading. I walked on. A steward in
uniform came running after me, stopped, bowed and then
indicated to me to follow him. I did and he led me to my
cabin. He brought me my luggage which I had left at the
gangway and disappeared. As I began to unpack, the man I

had seen in his underclothes came to my cabin. Now dressed in officer's uniform, he bowed and introduced himself as the first officer. He expressed a welcome on behalf of the captain. He informed me that I would be the only passenger. He then enquired if I would seek dinner ashore since the captain would be entertaining the ship's agent in the dining room. I had given notice to the office of the agent that I would be on the ship for dinner. Moreover there are no restaurants in the docks area so I informed the first officer that he could put me at a table in the corner of the dining room. I would be there only a short time and would not disturb the captain and his guest. He bowed and went off. Later the steward came to announce dinner. He led me to the dining room. It was empty and I dined alone. The captain, I later learned had gone ashore.

We sailed early in the morning, remaining in sight of land as we navigated the Straits of Malacca, rounded the northern tip of Sumatra, and out into the vast expanse of the Indian Ocean. The weather was fine and the sea was fairly calm. The sky was cloudless and at night the dark blue sky was filled with stars and our wake gleamed with phosphorescence. I dined in solitary state in the dining room. Two young engineers sought me out early in the voyage. They could speak some English and wished to practise it. They first met me on deck in the evening but later used to come to my cabin. They told me that they were accustomed to have their meals in the dining room but the captain had issued an order that none of the officers was to enter the dining room on this voyage. At night I paced the deck outside my cabin. Sometimes a young sailor, dressed only in a white brief loincloth, would come out on the foredeck below with a guitar and sing Japanese songs in a husky voice. One of these songs I found evocative and wistful. I wrote out the vocal melody and arranged a guitar and clarinet accompaniment. When in the following year I had occasion to visit Japan, I enquired about this song and obtained a recording. I was told the song was 'Wakare no Ipponsugi', a well-known song about a castle in the moonlight.

Our first port of call was Djibouti at the entrance to the Red Sea. The streets were sandy and the attempts at a garden in some of the few villas were notably unsuccessful. A sign 'A la plage' pointed to the beach and I optimistically followed it, thinking of taking a pleasant swim. The beach turned out to be a mud flat with a bistro on the shore where a jaded, heavily made-up Frenchwoman, presided with bored impassivity over an empty bar. Equally miserable was our next stop, the port of Massawa in Eritrea, where an Italian barber, a relic of the brief Italian colonial period, had a pathetic little shop. Port Sudan, a small town further up the coast, had a pleasant English-style hotel where I had dinner. There did not appear to be any guests in the hotel and the sea at the jetty was crystal clear. We then sailed across the Red Sea and called at Jiddah. A sentry from the Saudi Army was posted at the gangway, slovenly in dress and behaviour. He would not allow me to go down on to the jetty even though some of the crew went down and were playing handball. Large American cars drove on to the jetty from time to time and ladies, dressed in black flowing gowns from head to foot and with veiled faces, descended and walked about.

On we went, past Suez and through the canal to Alexandria, where we tied up alongside to discharge and take on a considerable amount of cargo. I visited the Montaza Palace, residence of the former King Farouk. Back on board the *New York Maru*, I had a fine view of the palace and took some photographs of it. Two destroyers were lying in front of it which had been purchased from Britain. This was the time of the Suez Crisis, which had just been nationalised by Colonel Nasser, the Egyptian head of state. Britain and France were threatening war and did in fact a few days later launch an attack on Egypt with a view to taking over the canal.

From Alexandria we sailed for Lattakia in Syria. It is a quiet little town but also appears to be a naval port. There were some small naval craft in the harbour. The harbour was too small for the *New York Maru*, which anchored some distance outside. The first officer said I could go ashore since they would not sail for some hours. A motorboat took me into the harbour where an officer in a uniform indicative of senior rank interviewed me, speaking in French, stamped my passport and graciously told me that Lattakia was mine. I walked through the town. There was little to see. There were one or two cafés with men seated outside drinking black coffee from tiny cups and smoking hookahs. After a few hundred yards I found myself on a pebble beach. I was glad of the exercise and walked briskly on this, leaving the town behind and looking out to sea where the *New York Maru* was visible in the distance. I came across a donkey on the beach. There was a man in the sea nearby. He was stark naked and appeared to be looking for shellfish.

When he saw me he assumed a suspicious expression, walked up to me and addressed me rather aggressively in Arabic. I indicated lack of comprehension. He spoke and gestured more aggressively and I had the impression that he was asking to see my passport. I was not disposed to produce this to him so finally he indicated that I should not move from the spot and took off with the donkey.

I was thinking that perhaps I might have a swim and eat the picnic lunch that the ship had provided me with but, before I could do this, an open lorry appeared with a number of armed soldiers at the back and stopped beside me. An officer got out from the cabin and approached me. He addressed me in French and asked what I was doing. I pointed out the *New York Maru* and told him that I was a passenger and was taking a walk for an hour or two while she was taking on cargo. He asked to see what was in the package I was carrying. I handed it to him: sandwiches. He asked me for my camera and I gave it to him. He then invited me to enter the cabin of the lorry beside the driver and he got in the back with the soldiers. We then drove off.

We arrived at a white-walled fort and drove through a narrow gate in the wall. I was conducted to a bare room with white-washed walls, devoid of furniture except for a table with a chair on either side. The soldiers from the lorry stood round the walls holding their rifles. I was asked to sit. A paper and pen were produced and another officer asked for my passport which I gave to him. It was a British passport. He then began to interrogate me in French and write down my answers in Arabic.

He told me that Britain was unfriendly to Syria. I replied that I was quite unaware of that and that Britain had diplomatic relations with Syria. Yes, he said, but Britain was now at war with Egypt and Egypt and Syria are sisters. He wanted to know exactly who I was and what I was doing there. He did not understand what was on my passport but he knew it was a British passport. He wanted to know my occupation. I was Crown Counsel, Sarawak. They had never heard of Sarawak. Had they heard of Borneo? No. Singapore? No. Malaya? No. I did not know how to translate Attorney General or Crown Counsel into French. I had a vague idea that in France there was a high official designated Procurateur Général who was responsible for all prosecutions. The best I could do then in description of occupation and location was to say that I was the Procurateur Général of Her Brittanic Majesty for the Far East. This, of course, was hardly an accurate translation of either Attorney General or Crown Counsel, Sarawak, but it was the nearest I could get, given my interrogator's limited knowledge of geography and my ignorance of the French equivalent of Attorney General or Crown Counsel. This statement had a visible effect although I could not judge just what the effect was.

The statement was recorded and I was asked to sign it. I pointed out that I could not read Arabic and did not know what I was being asked to sign. However the officer said a signature was necessary so I signed it and wrote in French above my signature that I signed because I was asked to sign but that I could not read Arabic and was therefore unaware of what was written above. I passed the statement back to the officer who read what I had written with a glimmer of a smile.

Then I was led back out into the courtyard. The officer invited me to face the high white wall. There were some stunted weeds at its foot and the officer asked me to look at the *flowers*. It was not clear to me why I should face the wall or look at the weeds. There was nothing much to look at. I turned round and was surprised to see all the soldiers lined up facing me a few yards away. They were standing to attention, holding their rifles. The officer stood at their side looking at me. It looked remarkably like a firing squad. I commended myself to God's mercy and resolved to uphold the honour of the British Empire and die with dignity. I waited for the word of command from the officer. Just then an open jeep pulled into the courtyard and stopped between me and the squad. It was driven by a soldier. The officer gestured to me to get in the back. He barked out a word of command, the jeep began to move and the soldiers presented arms in General Salute. I returned the salute by taking off my hat and bowing graciously breathed a sigh of relief. Presumably the honour was for Her Brittanic Majesty's Procurateur Général for the Far East and to avoid a diplomatic contretemps.

The jeep took me back to the harbour and left me with the senior officer who had told me on arrival that Lattakia was mine. He looked at me sadly. 'You ventured into a prohibited military zone.' I expressed astonishment and ignorance. I had been on an empty beach with no sign of military installations. Nor had I seen any notices of any sort. I reminded him that I was a stranger and when he welcomed me to Lattakia he indicated that I could go anywhere and did not inform me that I should not go on to the beach. He said no more but gave me the sandwiches which had been taken from me and the camera. He asked me for the film in the camera. Then I remembered that it contained a photograph of the Montaza Palace which had two destroyers of the Egyptian Navy lying in front of it. This could be misconstrued. I took care not to rewind the film into its cassette but simply opened the back of the camera and took out the film, now totally exposed and its photographs obliterated. A naval launch was waiting to take me back to the *New York Maru*.

We sailed for Salonika. As we neared it the ship's doctor came to me and said that this was the first time that an NYK ship had called at Salonika and the captain wished to invite various local notabilities there to come aboard for cocktails. The captain wished to make a speech to them in English. Would I write the speech for him? I agreed and wrote what I thought might be appropriate things to say. I gave the speech to the doctor. I had thought that I might be invited to the party and at last get to see the captain. I had spoken with some of the officers but had never met the captain. I was not invited to the party nor did I see the captain. When we reached Istanbul and I was about to disembark, the first officer came to me and presented me with a cigarette lighter enamelled with the flag of the NYK line. This, he said, was a gift from the captain who regretted that he had been very busy on the voyage and had been unable to meet me. Perhaps I had not been forgiven for choosing to dine aboard in Singapore.

The Case of the Timber Tycoon and the Rising Star from Singapore

Sarawak was at this time thickly forested with magnificent trees over a hundred feet high—primeval forest, never felled. To travel in it was an unforgettable experience; the smell of fecundity, the atmosphere of stillness and the sense of the passage of millions of years had created a unique ambience. However, the government had to utilize such resources as it had in order to create revenue which would make the colony viable. The British Government, which somewhat reluctantly accepted the cession of the territory from the third and last Rajah, Sir Charles Vyner Brooke, had its own financial problems and was not prepared to expend its revenues on Sarawak. Timber, then, had to be harvested. Conservation was unheard of in those days. Ramin, the Malay name for a species of dipterocarp, the giant forest tree, was a popular import for those countries in need of timber for their furniture industries and Sarawak had an abundant supply. However the very abundance of the supply—and Sarawak was not the only country with ramin forests—drove the prices down and the government imposed a ban on export to be maintained until prices rose to a sufficient level.

During this ban, I had a visit from a Yugoslav captain of a large Yugoslav freighter docked at one of our major ports. After preliminary courtesies, he informed me that he was an expert in maritime law and was in fact a judge of the Yugoslav maritime court. Interesting as this might be, it could hardly be the reason for him to take the time to see me. After expressing suitable recognition of his expertise in law and judicial standing I waited for him to proceed. Proceed he did. The reason for his visit was that the customs department had detained his ship. It was a ten-thousand-ton vessel and was fully loaded with timber, ready to depart. The demurrage—the financial loss attributable to delay—was very substantial and it was imperative that the ship be allowed to depart immediately in order to avoid causing this loss. Moreover the ship had other commitments to meet elsewhere and a fixed timetable. Presumably, I suggested, the customs department considered that they had reason to detain the ship. Well, yes, he said. They were alleging that the ship was loaded with ramin but it was in fact loaded with mixed light hardwoods, which were freely exportable. But, surely, I suggested, the customs department, who had at their disposal the advice of the forestry department, were aware of the difference in appearance between ramin and mixed light hardwoods. He did not dispute that. What the customs department were saying, he told me, was that the top layer, the visible layer of timber, was mixed light hardwoods but that everything under that was ramin. They wanted him to unload so that they could prove this. Unloading would take at least ten days and involve a huge sum in demurrage. I told him that I was in no position to adjudicate on whether the customs were justified or not. Unloading would settle the dispute one way or another. The captain was not satisfied. He wanted to get away as soon as possible. The timber was not his concern but he was responsible for the ship and its commitments which did not permit of it being detained for ten days in Sarawak and possibly another ten days re-loading. I pointed out to him that there might be a way out. The customs and the forestry departments obviously had some reason to think that the shipment was almost entirely ramin in disguise. If they were correct in their views there would be heavy penalties incurred by the exporters. To prove their views were correct, customs and forestry needed evidence. Unloading would, if their views were correct, provide that evidence. The evidence could be provided in another way. The captain was not an expert on timber and might not know the difference between various species. The exporters would know very well what species they were exporting. The export was their responsibility and to their profit. If the exporters chose to admit that the shipment was indeed ramin, there would be no need to detain the ship. I emphasized to him that I was not demanding or even requesting such an admission. The exporters knew what timber was in the ship and they were free to say what they pleased. If they denied the accusation, then the ship would be unloaded and if the official view was wrong and the shipment was indeed mixed light hardwoods then the government would have to accept liability for wrongful detention and pay appropriate compensation. The captain departed to see the exporters.

A few days later the Controller of Customs informed me that the exporters had delivered to the customs department a statutory declaration made by the managing director of the exporters that the shipment was indeed of ramin. I instructed the Controller to allow the vessel to depart.

This was no small matter. The shipment was very large and involved violations of several sections of the Forestry Ordinance and also the Customs Ordinance. These carried possible sentences of imprisonment and also fines calculated as a substantial multiple of the value of the timber. I framed the charges and the managing director of the exporters, Mr Lau, was duly charged in the High Court in Sibu, the provincial capital of the area of the port where the ship was loaded. The charges caused a stir since the managing director was a very wealthy man, a tycoon of the timber industry, with a prominent place in society. The essence of the matter was fraud. He had tried to make a substantial amount of money by deceit as well as flouting a law passed for the economic benefit of the country. His reputation in the eyes of those of his fellows in the business community who had a moral sense, would suffer in the event of a conviction. It would also suffer in the eyes of those unburdened with moral principles but who had hitherto credited him with being adroit in his ways of doing business. What with this consideration and the prospect of prison and an enormous fine, the accused set about procuring for himself the very best in the way of defence counsel.

In Singapore the rising star was Lee Kuan Yew. He subsequently became the architect of the new post-colonial Singapore and with a team of able colleagues converted it into a modern and prosperous city-state and became world famous as a statesman gifted with unusually perspicuous insight into world affairs and the science of government. He had had an outstanding academic career and at this time was making a name for himself as a powerful and persuasive advocate as well as a brilliant lawyer. These are not the same thing. There are good advocates who do not have the intellectual equipment to be really good lawyers. And one can have excellent lawyers who have no gift of advocacy, which includes eloquence and the ability to think quickly on one's feet. Lee Kuan Yew had a superlative intellect, he had the gift of lucid exposition of a case, making what was complex simple to understand, he had a rapier-like mind capable of dealing with the unexpected twists and turns which can occur in court as a result of unforeseen changes in a witness's testimony or a question from the court, and he was never impatient or excited or flustered, no matter what happened, but always calm and clear. This was Mr Lau's choice as his counsel and he could not have chosen better.

On the flight to Sibu for the trial—by this time a regular air service between Kuching and Sibu had been established—I found that the seat beside me was occupied by a grave-looking gentleman whom I did not know. This gentleman, I observed, was glancing at me from time to time, but I thought it prudent to keep my attention fixed on the current issue of the law journal I had brought to read on the plane. I was not altogether surprised to find when I got to court the next day that the gentleman was Mr Lau. It would be charitable to assume that the seating arrangement was a coincidence.

When I arrived at the courthouse the following day I was met by a disciplined array of boys and girls in Chinese school uniform. Singapore was still a colony at that time but it had a legislative assembly in which Mr Lee was the leading critic of the colonial government. His speeches and interventions were fully reported in the press. Although invariably polite he was incisive, satirical and, on occasion, devastating. The officials sitting on the official side of the assembly were dull by comparison, were skillfully made to sound defensive and, if any of them took refuge in pomposity, his pomposity was swiftly punctured by a shaft of wit, which amused the opposition and was secretly relished by their colleagues. The Chinese schools in Sarawak who were not enamoured of colonial government regarded him with the adulation later accorded, with less reason, to popstars and football players. During the hearing in Sibu, school groups came into the courtroom, sat down to watch their hero, went out again and were replaced by the next group. During the trial their hero was given a grand dinner by the Hakka community—Mr Lee was a Hakka—to which the Resident and I were also courteously invited. We were happy to attend.

The senior magistrate presided over the trial. He was a Welshman with strict views on propriety. I opened the proceedings by introducing my learned friend Mr Lee as counsel for the accused and his junior who was assisting him. I outlined the circumstances which were the occasion for the trial and explained the nature of the charges against the accused and read the relevant sections of the Customs Ordinance and the Forestry Ordinance and those provisions of the subsidiary legislation made under them which were applicable to the facts which I hoped to prove. Having done this I then called witnesses from the two departments concerned. They deposed to the arrival of the ship, the loading of the ship, the tonnage loaded and the number of days involved. They then related their reasons for detaining the ship and what had led them to believe that the timber loaded, apart from a light sprinkling of mixed light hardwoods on top, was ramin. To establish that their belief was correct, the master of the ship was ordered to unload. The Controller of Customs subsequently countermanded this order and the ship was allowed to sail without inspection of the cargo. This called for explanation.

Attorney General (A.G.): Can you tell the court why you countermanded your order and allowed the ship to sail?

Controller: The exporter came to my office.

A.G.: Who was the exporter?

Controller: Mr Lau.

A.G.: Can you identify him?

Controller: Yes. (Points out the accused.)

A.G.: Why did he come to see you?

Controller: He came to tell me that the cargo was, as we had reason to believe, ramin and asked me whether since he was not now disputing it the ship could sail.

A.G.: What was your reply to this?

Controller: I referred the question to the Attorney General's chambers and was informed that if the accused's statement was made in the form of a statutory declaration and was in unequivocal terms the ship could be allowed to sail if I so permitted. Since the ramin had already been cut and the penalties which would be incurred would be very considerable I was prepared to allow the ramin to go.

A.G.: What did you tell the accused?

Controller: I told him that his verbal statement was insufficient and informed him of the advice that I had received.

A.G.: Had you asked the accused to come to your office on the occasion when he told you the shipment was ramin?

Controller: No.

A.G.: Did you have any communication with the accused about this shipment before he came to your office?

Controller: Yes. On information received from my officers at the port I ordered the detention of the ship. I then had a telephone call from Mr Lau protesting about the order. I told him the order would stand and that the ship had to be unloaded.

A.G.: What happened after you informed the accused of the advice you had received from the Attorney General's chambers?

Controller: I telephoned him with the advice and some time later he came to my office with the statutory declaration.

A.G.: Are you familiar with the Statutory Declarations Ordinance?

Controller: Yes. We ask for statutory declarations from importers and exporters from time to time since it is impossible for us to search every consignment thoroughly and we have to rely on statutory declarations.

A.G.: You accepted the statutory declaration?

Controller: Yes, it was in proper form.

A.G.: Can you produce it now?

Controller: Yes. (He produces the declaration. It was made before a magistrate on solemn affirmation. There is a declaration at the end that all the contents are true and that the deponent, Mr Lau, is aware that it is a criminal offence to make a false declaration. It contained the statement that the timber loaded by Mr Lau is entirely ramin except for a few mixed light hardwood logs.)

The next witness was the magistrate who received the declaration.

Attorney General (A.G.): Do you know Mr Lau the accused in this case?

Magistrate: I know him now.

A.G.: When did you first come to know him?

Magistrate: I first came to know him when he arrived at my chambers and informed my clerk that he wished to affirm a statutory declaration before me.

A.G.: What did you do?

Magistrate: I asked my clerk to show him in.

A.G.: And then?

Magistrate: My clerk showed him in. He announced his name and told me that he had prepared a form of statutory declaration and wished to affirm it before me.

A.G.: Was there any customs or forestry officer around?

Magistrate. No.

A.G.: Were there any government officers or police around your court at the time?

Magistrate: No, there were not.

A.G.: Did you read the declaration?

Magistrate: Yes, I read it aloud.

A.G.: Why did you read it aloud?

Magistrate: It was a statement which revealed that the deponent was contravening the law and I wished him to be quite clear about what he was stating.

A.G.: Do you know if the accused was aware that it is an offence to make a false statement in a statutory declaration?

Magistrate: The declaration by the deponent specifically said that he was aware of this and I expressly drew his attention to this before he affirmed it.

A.G.: What happened then?

Magistrate: He signed the declaration in my presence. He signed two copies, one of which I retained for my records, the other he took away.

A.G.: Have you any further information about this matter?

Magistrate: That is all I know.

That concluded the case for the Crown. Counsel for the accused had not cross-examined the prosecution witnesses. He now addressed the court and said that the defence would be that the statement on which the Crown case depended was obtained by duress and was therefore inadmissible as evidence. Statements extracted from any person by force are rightly suspect as being of dubious veracity and are thus, under the law relating to evidence, unacceptable in proceedings in court. Mr Lau was then called to the witness box. He related that he had loaded many tons of timber, he told us the exact quantity, over ten days. When the loading was complete and the ship was ready to sail, an order was made by the Controller of Customs prohibiting the departure of the ship. Mr Lau was immediately notified by the ship's captain. He contacted the customs at once and was informed that they wanted the ship unloaded since they were of the belief that the timber loaded was ramin, the export of which was prohibited. He protested that the timber was all mixed light hardwoods but the customs were adamant. If the ship was detained he would be liable for the demurrage and this was likely to amount to a very large sum. The ship was a ten-thousand-ton vessel. Unloading could take ten days or more and he would be faced with a huge financial claim. He was told by the Controller that the ship could sail if he made a statutory declaration that the shipment was ramin. He had no choice. He made the declaration. However the shipment contained no ramin, he claimed, but only what was stated in the customs export declaration, namely mixed light hardwoods.

It was then my turn to cross-examine.

Attorney General (A.G.): Had you ever visited the Controller's office before you went there with the statutory declaration?

Lau: No.

A.G.: Did he ask you to make the declaration?

Lau: He told me the ship could sail if I made the statutory declaration.

A.G.: This was after you had previously called at his office telling him that the timber was ramin.

Lau: (reluctantly) Yes.

A.G.: Can we get the sequence right? You first contacted the Controller about this shipment by telephone to protest about the detention order?

Lau: Yes.

A.G.: He told you that the order would stand and the ship had to be unloaded?

Lau: Yes.

A.G.: Your next contact with the Controller was when you went to see him?

Lau: Yes.

A.G.: You have heard his evidence. He said that you told him that the timber which had been loaded was ramin, that you were no longer disputing this and that you wanted the detention order countermanded on that basis.

Lau: Yes.

A.G.: Your visit to him was at your own desire?

Lau: Well I felt I had to see him.

A.G.: The visit was not at his invitation?

Lau: No.

A.G.: Your visit was at your wish, not his.

Lau: I suppose so.

A.G.: No, Mr Lau, this is not a supposition. You went there because you wanted to see him not because he has asked to see you.

Lau: Yes.

A.G.: As far as the Controller was concerned he had ordered that the ship should be unloaded?

Lau: Yes.

A.G.: You went to see him with the object of getting him to reverse his order?

Lau: Yes.

A.G.: And your way of achieving this was to admit what the customs suspected, namely that the shipment was indeed ramin?

Lau: Yes but it wasn't ramin.

A.G.: That is what you now say but you told the Controller it was ramin.

Lau: Yes because I felt I had no choice.

A.G.: We will come to the question of choice later. The Controller told you a verbal statement was not enough and there had to be a statutory declaration?

Lau: Yes.

A.G.: Had you made statutory declarations before in course of your export business?

Lau: A few times.

A.G.: You understand that they are intended to be solemnly affirmed documents and that their contents must be true?

Lau (very reluctantly): I believe so.

A.G.: You believe so? Did you not expressly state in the declaration that the contents were true?

Lau: That is what it said in the declaration?

A.G.: It is your declaration, is it not?

Lau: I had no choice.

A.G.: That is no answer to the question. You made this declaration on solemn affirmation before the magistrate. Do you deny that?

Lau : No.

A.G.: And you are now saying that it contained a deliberate lie?

Lau: I had no choice.

A.G.: You have told us that before. You are evading the issue which is that you now wish the court to believe that the statutory declaration is a massive and calculated lie.

Lau: What could I do?

A.G.: You were free to stick to your story that the timber was mixed light hardwoods.

Lau: Then the ship would have to be unloaded and I as the shipper would be liable to the ship owners for huge demurrage.

A.G.: You are an experienced businessman, Mr Lau. You know perfectly well that if the timber consisted of mixed light hardwoods and the customs had wrongly ordered the unloading you would be entitled to call upon the government to pay the demurrage and any other loss you suffered?

Lau: I didn't think of that.

A.G.: You thought of making a lying declaration but you, a businessman of long experience, did not think of telling the Controller that you would hold him liable for the loss caused by what you now allege was an order which had no factual basis?

Lau: (no answer)

A.G.: Are you telling the court, having demonstrated that you are quite prepared to lie when it suits you and you think you can obtain some advantage, that your testimony now, when your declaration if it stands, exposes you to heavy penalties, is true?

Lau: I am speaking the truth.

A.G.: Isn't that what you said to the magistrate and now you tell us you weren't?

There was no answer and none was necessary.

Counsel for Mr Lau did not re-examine. He closed his case and addressed the Court. The sole hope of the defence was the plea of duress. If the statutory declaration was extracted from Mr Lau by duress then it was inadmissible in evidence and that was the end of the Crown case since there would now be no evidence that the timber was ramin. It might also be difficult to mount a charge of perjury when the document containing the perjury would be inadmissible because of the duress and Mr Lau could be counted on to deny that he ever told the Controller that the shipment was ramin. Mr Lee expounded the law on duress with his customary clarity, eloquence and erudition. The case laws which he cited told us all about duress and illustrated the principle in action in various circumstances. He passed rather more lightly over the facts.

In reply, I had to point out that none of the cases cited by Mr Lee were based on facts which resembled in any way the facts in the present case. Customs did not force Mr Lau to make his declaration. The Controller had made an order in exercise of his lawful powers. He wanted the order complied with. It was Mr Lau who didn't want the order complied with and in order to avoid complying with it chose to go to the Controller and admit that the shipment was ramin. The Controller did not ask him to admit this. He himself chose to go and see the Controller and tell him. The Controller was not prepared to accept a mere verbal statement which could later be denied and informed Mr Lau that his statement would be acceptable only in the form of a statutory declaration. Mr Lau was under no compulsion to make a statutory declaration any more than he was under compulsion to go and see the Controller and admit to the shipment. This was done at his own desire because he did not want the ship unloaded. If it were unloaded and revealed to be ramin, the Controller might well have ordered confiscation of the ramin, Mr Lau would be faced with the loss of the very valuable shipment, he would face criminal charges of deceit and attempted violation of the laws and in addition he would be liable to the ship owners for the very substantial demurrage incurred. Now that the ship is gone he feels that he is free to repudiate the declaration which he had previously solemnly declared to be true before a magistrate and signed the declaration accordingly. He hopes that by doing so he will get off scot-free and have the profits from the ramin shipment as well. Mr Lau is a liar by his own admission. There was no duress as that term is defined in law and in the authorities on duress. His plea should be rejected.

There was then a brief adjournment. When the magistrate returned he delivered his judgement. He rejected the plea of duress as being unfounded in law and fact, he found the accused guilty of all the charges under the customs and Forestry Ordinances. The penalties under the Customs Ordinance alone, being a multiple of the value of the timber, amounted to by far the largest fine ever imposed by a court in Sarawak. In addition, since this was not simply a case of transgression of these statutes but involved shameless and deliberate deceit, he imposed a sentence of imprisonment of two years.

In the vestibule of the court Lee Kuan Yew stopped me to tell me how mistaken in law the magistrate was and to repeat his arguments on duress. I had to say that I was not the judge and there was little point in him repeating what I had already heard him say in court. I acknowledged that he had done all that could be done for his client but I could not agree with his submission. He announced that he would appeal. Appeal he did to the High Court where the arguments were heard again but in vain for the appellant. Judgement and the sentence were upheld.

The sentence of imprisonment came as a great shock to the accused and to the business community in which he was prominent. He would have been better advised to adhere to his declaration when the Court would have been given evidence of a transgression of the export law and a free admission of this by the accused. He would have been fined according to the provisions of the various laws involved but in view of the free admission of his guilt and the very heavy fines it is perhaps unlikely that he would have been sentenced to imprisonment. However the case had a salutary effect on exporters who now knew what to expect if they tried to deceive the customs.

Fishing with the
Melanau of Sarawak

The District Officer of the Melanau area of Sarawak sent me what was intended to be a definitive code of the customary law of the Melanau people. The Melanau are a racial group living on the coast of Sarawak with their own distinctive customs and their own social hierarchy. They are mostly fishing folk and, unlike the rest of the population, have sago and not rice as their staple food. Melanau were formerly very much under the rule and influence of Brunei, with distinctive customary laws regulating much of their personal affairs and hierarchical social system. Since there were differences of opinion amongst the leaders of the various subdistricts as to these laws, the District Officer had creditably set himself, in discussion with these leaders, to resolve the differences and come up with an agreed statement of the law. Unfortunately when I studied this document there seemed to be considerable ambiguity. I decided to go to the area and spend some time there with the leaders discussing the ambiguities. This was a change from my usual run of duties.

I obtained a launch from the Director of Marine and

sailed for Oya on the northern coast. The jetty for Oya was situated just inland on the bank of a river. The mouth of the Oya river is practically indistinguishable from the sea but the eagle eyes of the master of the launch picked it out and his skilful navigation brought us through the tricky channels to the jetty where Datu Pengiran Lai, the area headman, together with the village headman and local notabilities were waiting. They came aboard and sat on deck, taking refreshments, while my kit was borne off and we sat chatting under the scrutiny of a crowd on the jetty. After courtesies were properly and unhurriedly exchanged they departed and it was now my turn to disembark and pay a courtesy call on Datu Pengiran Lai. His house was full of villagers sitting crosslegged on the floor. I was given a chair. An elaborate formal speech of welcome was made by the Datu and I replied in the same elaborate and formal vein. At this stage the son of the village headman, a handsome young man, approached with a brass tray. He knelt in front of me and offered the tray to me. On it there was a blue and white bowl which I recognized as Ming export ware, exported in junks from China to Borneo three hundred years before. The bowl contained what looked like roast caterpillars. These are the toredo worm, notorious for boring into the hulls of wooden seagoing vessels. The Melanau, who eat sago and not rice, take a sago trunk, sink it in a river near the sea and leave it there for months. When they retrieve it, it is full of the toredo worm, which they bake or roast and esteem as a delicacy. I was dismayed to be offered a bowl of these but with all eyes upon me I felt obliged, as a matter of courtesy, to pick one up, put it in my mouth and hastily swallow it. Everyone was watching with interest. The penghulu said: 'Do you like these?' 'Er, yes, delicious,' I replied, with less than the truth. 'Well, do have some more!' he said. Later they said to me that I was the first non-Melanau ever to appreciate the toredo. This was a distinction I could have done without.

In recognition of my appreciation of their delicacy they gave me an empty cigarette tin filled with them. I offered this to the Malay master of the launch and my offer was politely but firmly declined.

I had to go upriver to pay a visit to the little township of Dalat. The bazaar of Dalat was old, dilapidated and drab. There were no roads in Dalat. This was essentially a riverine village and without a sampan, one was practically immobile. Sampans darted everywhere, propelled with dignified elan by everyone from 4-year-olds to stately septuagenarian matrons chaste in black with gold buttons. At night, the sampans have a pressure lamp in the bows and the blackness of the river is dotted with gliding points of light.

At Dalat there is a large keliding, an ancient burial monument of uncertain age. It seems to be made of bilian, Bornean ironwood, but the years have worn away its carvings and it is greatly weathered. About four or five feet up, there is a large hole where the bones of persons of high rank were placed after the flesh decayed. It was formerly the custom to tie a live slave to the top and leave him to die of heat, thirst and starvation.

The procedure of the Dalat parish council which I had

come to attend, was of a high grace. The Datu presided majestically and conducted the proceedings with regal tact. Melanau elders rose, made their points in stately Malay with a balance, precision and polish worthy of Queen's Counsel. The clerk was the very model of a clerk; quiet and unobtrusive but every letter and every minute was produced at precisely the right moment and every point that required to be made was made under his discreet guidance. The administrative officer, emissary of the District Officer whose seat was a considerable distance away by river and sea, had briefed himself thoroughly on the agenda and had the relevant law and policy at his finger tips. Differences of opinion were indicated in the most diplomatic fashion and were equally diplomatically and smoothly resolved. Members of more prominent councils might derive much advantage from observing these proceedings.

Back in Oya I cycled from Oya to Mukah for a district council meeting. The road lay along the beach; to be more accurate, it was the beach. At various points, signs to landward marked 'In' and 'Out' indicated the sections of road leading over streams impassable by bicycle at high tide. At the major rivers—Buloh, Penat, Judan and Petanak—it was necessary to go inland over an arc of road hung over with tall trees and, in the case of Penat and Judan, lined with meadows, a refreshing sight after the exposed beach and the shimmering sea. Penat, with its green fields and scattered houses had an air of rural England. The villagers were sturdy fishing folk unaffected by modern ideas and styles. The Sungei Buloh road by night was silent and eerie with trees narrowly hemming the road and overhanging it. The area had a wandering restless ghost of which many stories were told. They were unauthenticated but this is irrelevant to the local people who do not possess the prosaic mind and are free from the thirst for fact which the West has acquired (though only in its more educated representatives) in relatively recent times. Truth can be understood in many ways as Pontius Pilate knew and fact, although its importance should not be underrated, is not necessarily a synonym.

Back once again in Oya it was 4.30 a.m. when a soft voice from outside the little house where I was staying summoned me out to the beach. The morning air was chilly on the estuary and the sea encompassed us like an endless carpet of grey silk. A light breeze bellied the square sail of the rolling fishing boat and we ploughed through the sea away into nothingness. The crew was comfortably lolling against the thwarts, drinking tea and eating cakes out of rusty tins. I declined the offer of a share, having breakfasted before leaving my house, and this confirmed everybody's expectation that I was going to be seasick.

Several miles out a hundred or so coconut fronds were anchored and, if we were lucky, pomfret and other fish would be basking in their shade. Panau fishing involves letting a large scoop net down on the starboard side of the boat, then hauling in a frond towards the vessel by a line at the end of which is a wooden decoy fish. Any fish under the frond follow it until they are over the net. Meanwhile two divers are out on the ends of the scoop. They submerge and pull the scoop down, heeling the boat almost onto her beam. When the fish are over the net, the scoops are released, those aboard leap to the port side and the net comes rapidly out of the sea with its catch. It is not an arduous method of fishing—it is suited only to calm weather—and no one does much work apart from the divers and the master, on whom the success of the voyage largely depends. Back in the estuary, sampans driven by outboard motors came dashing alongside the fishing boat and the surplus fish were weighed and borne off to a launch filled with ice. The takings were divided amongst the boat (two shares), the engine (one and a half), the master (two shares) and the crew (one share each). There are usually about thirteen people in a boat but the number varies.

By eight o'clock the sun was fierce, beating like a hammer on the brazen sea. We were wearing terendak, wide circular hats made of palm leaves, but the heat was trying nonetheless and when we stopped at ten to have a meal, tattered pieces of leaf matting were produced and little tents sprang up on the deck. With the aid of heavy razor-sharp knives, pomfret and other fish were cleaned and sliced with the easy, beautiful precision of a surgeon. The slices were paper thin and there were three different sauces to dip them in. With a squeeze of lime juice and a handful of sago pearls, they made a meal which Prunier might have envied.

The other method of fishing, requiring communal effort, is known as rantau. This involves laying a long dragnet some distance from the shore and parallel to the beach. At each end is a very long rope and a team of about seven men waist-deep in the sea haul the net into a great semicircle centred on the beach. Each man has a rope round his waist which he hitches onto the net-rope. He hauls this backward until he is well up the beach, unhitches and goes forward into the sea and repeats the process. The whole operation takes about an hour and a half. Everyone wears a long-sleeved shirt, rubber or leather gauntlets and two pairs of old trousers caught at the ankles by a pair or two pairs of rolled stockings. The clothing offers some protection against jellyfish and ikan sembilang, a kind of catfish notorious for the poisonous wound inflicted by the serrated spines of its dorsal and pectoral fins. Orange-coloured jellyfish are very common and give a nasty sting. An astonishing ragbag of fish is caught by this method. A few days before I witnessed this, a huge sawfish weighing twenty kilos was in the collection.

In the shallow sea between Kuala Matu and Kuala Oya were the jermal and kilong, put up by the three fishing kongsi centred on Kuala Matu. The principle of the jermal is two converging rows of stakes, carefully sited with an eye to currents and tides, leading to a narrow passage where a large scoop net is situated. When the tide is setting into the passage, it is hoped a stream of fish will enter. The stakes vibrate in the water and the fish tend to stay in the centre of the passage and, since it is not their habit to turn and flee, they soon find themselves on the waiting scoop net.

The kilong is similar to the jermal but the passage leads into a wire-netting enclosure from which the fish cannot escape. The kilong has the advantage that it goes on trapping fish all the time whereas the jermal requires someone to be there to operate it.

Both these types of trap suffer in bad weather. The stakes may be swept away or the matrix ruined. This worries jermal proprietors more than kilong proprietors since the former do not generally fare so well as the latter. In fact rantau fishermen will tell you that they can do better than any jermal. The rantau fisherman has the advantage that his capital outlay is small, he is mobile and can follow the fish and when there are no fish he can employ himself more usefully in cultivation of crops.

Weddings, Affairs
and Exorcisms

The Matu River is very narrow and is bounded on either side by flat land where rice and this being Melanau territory, sago, are planted. Between the estuary and Matu there is little of note save Kampong Sok where there was one of the few remaining Melanau longhouses. It was a very old building but in good repair. Unlike the Iban longhouse, it had no exterior verandah and a long, high wide central corridor served the purpose of the Iban interior verandah. The corridor, the floor of which was of solid plank timber, was dim since the only source of light was a window at either end. On each side were thirteen rooms, notable for the fact that they had no doors and the passer-by was at liberty to inspect the entire interior. The population of this house was a hundred and sixty and it was a clean and pleasant place. The dogs, chickens, cocks, pigs and other variegated animal life, which mark the Iban longhouse, were absent and by comparison the Melanau house seemed curiously lifeless.

Matu has a bright, spacious air: flat, open, grassy country with the weedy river flowing softly through it. The flat banks are frequently under water and the only road is a plank or gangway on timber pillars running airily from the shophouses downriver, up past the Government office and, the police and government quarters to the upper bridge leading to the village. Moored at the government wharf was an old launch, converted with considerable imagination into a houseboat and decorated with taste.

From Matu come fine conical hats of woven bamboo in natural colours, embroidered with beads and silver wire and with a silver corona at their apex. Bright flowers and stars are the most frequent contemporary theme of the embroidery but the classical design consists of simple crosses arranged in a pattern. The best hats were made by the wife and daughter of the headman, Abang Abdul Ghani, a man of distinguished manners.

The river up to Kampong Tian was, at the time, no more than six feet wide and a foot deep but the surrounding country became a lake during the rains. The village was built on very high piles in consequence. Of considerable antiquity, it contained many small longhouses of sixty or seventy souls living in each vast open apartment. The teeming life of the village was its most attractive feature. The people were renowned for their handsome appearance: smooth skin the colour of honey and classic proportions. The women were said to be the most beautiful in Sarawak.

The rasping of sago was still done by hand here and the method of treading the sago differed from that employed elsewhere. Instead of spreading the pith on a square mat to be trodden by one or two persons, it was put in a large rattan basket and the person treading it stepped inside the basket and rotated in a slow-motion shuffling pirouette.

Back in Matu, a large crowd had turned up to listen to a tale of human frailty being unfolded in the district court. An elderly gentleman with a younger wife found her in *flagrante delicto* with their lusty, young lodger in a rubber garden. The elderly gentleman, enraged and affronted, whipped out his machete and managed to slash the lodger on the arm before he fled with the wife. That might have been the end of the matter but the husband, righteously indignant, went to complain to the police. There he learnt that law and morality are not the same thing and, to his astonishment and indignation, he was charged with voluntarily causing hurt with a cutting instrument.

The young police prosecutor called the lodger, a handsome youth of patrician appearance in a black velvet Malay cap, as his first witness and elicited the incredible story that the witness and the wife were simply standing talking when the husband arrived and for no reason attacked the witness with a machete. Having thus laid the foundation of his case, the inexperienced prosecutor then began to cross-examine the witness on the basis that his evidence was untrue! The witness was clearly unused to telling lies but he adhered to his original evidence.

The wife, pretty but in a frigid sulk, was called next and she refused to take the oath or be affirmed. The magistrate asked her if she was unwilling to give evidence against her husband.

She replied that she was perfectly willing to give evidence but she was not prepared to swear or affirm that it was true! That disposed of her as a witness and the case shakily proceeded over to the defence. The accused told his story with simplicity and patent sincerity. When he had finished, no one was in any doubt as to the truth of the matter except, apparently, the young prosecutor, whose first question in cross-examination was: 'What reason do you think your wife could have had to do this with this man?'

Unfortunately, an official engagement prevented me from hearing the answer to this interesting question. The distinguished 60-year-old patriarch who accompanied me stayed to hear the rest. Telling me about it afterwards he clicked his tongue disapprovingly and said: 'Naked in a rubber plantation! These people are like animals!' He himself had just married a 20-year-old girl a month or so before.

There was an exorcism ceremony going on in a house in Kampong Baharu at Oya on the night of my return. The patient was a girl who lived in a world of her own. She was nubile and pretty but, on this occasion, grievously distressed. The healer was a middle-aged gentleman from Dalat whose powers were renowned. The girl sat in the centre of the floor with her hair loose about her shoulders and her face while the operator chanted, largely unintelligibly. He stroked the girl's body with stalks of padi, took empty cigarette tins, chanted spells into them, placed them on the girl's head and various parts of her body, and after more spells, plucked them sharply from her and cast them out of the window. From time to time he expressed a feeling of hunger and was given glowing charcoal, which he champed with exaggerated satisfaction. The crowd thought this an amusing parlour trick but were unimpressed. They were interested to see whether the girl would benefit from her treatment. Sometimes they do and sometimes they don't. It depends on the strength of the spirit possessing them and the will of Allah.

Outside two of the houses in Kampong Tillian Ulu hung a large variety of colourful flags including standards proudly indicating the rank of the occupants. Old Brunei cannon lined the gangway from the floating jetty to the house. Everyone was dressed in their finery, the men in songkok, the Malay velvet cap, and short sarong over their trousers and with golden sovereign buttons on their shirts.

Below, two masked grotesques were miming in the undergrowth, issuing forth to pursue small boys who fled with screams of mingled terror and delight.

The elders in the house sat round in a large circle facing the crimson pelmet and screen, with intricate gold tracery and other decorations adorning the alcove containing the nuptial couch. In front of the screen, in a row, sat three grave elders, the representatives of the bride's family, waiting to receive and inspect the formal customary gifts presented by the family of the groom. Presently the beating of gongs was heard, a perahu drew up to the jetty and a procession of the groom's representatives mounted the jetty and entered the house, bearing the betrothal and bridal gifts: an ornamented spear, gold, a coconut, a sword, more gold, a wooden bowl, a gold-thread handkerchief and a piece of old Chinese pottery.

They entered the house looking subdued and, with gestures of self-deprecating politeness, the first personage bowed to the bride's representatives and sat cross-legged before them. The real discussion over dowry and the other gifts had taken place before and a settlement had been agreed but there was still a little room for manoeuvre and skilful, witty negotiators experienced in the customary code are much in demand. However, the occasion was public and momentous; honour must be preserved and courtesy maintained. At the same time, adroit fencing could win public sympathy and support and an advantage be gained over the other side. Behind their grave and impassive demeanour the negotiators keyed themselves up and the spectators prepared to enjoy themselves.

'These bangles are very fine but is their weight not somewhat light? Would it not be proper to add another?'

'Their weight in the hand is a thing of the mind. In the scales they are true. However in view of the extent of the sago-gardens given in dowry, generous even for a bride of such notably distinguished descent, it would not be unreasonable to proffer bridal gifts a fraction less than custom normally demands.'

The procession came and went and came again. One by one gifts were presented, examined and discussed with many sly thrusts on either side. At length the bride's representatives declared themselves satisfied and issued an invitation for the groom, sitting all the while unhappily at home. A small flotilla of boats accompanied him on his journey, flags flying and gongs and drums beating. In the centre of his boat he sat wearing an embroidered songkok and jacket, with serious face and moving not a muscle. Nine flags indicating his high rank flew from his standard. His eyes were modestly cast down and in his hand he held a handkerchief. His best man took the other end of the handkerchief and conducted him through the crowd of guests and spectators into the house where the bride, a beauty whose radiance was dimmed by the embarrassment of the occasion into a look of unwonted petulance, sat on one of twin thrones. The groom, casting not so much as a glance in her direction, was led to the other throne, seated and their hands were limply and reluctantly joined.

The art of conversation has not, in the East, suffered the decline that it has in the West and the Tuan Imam, the tua kampong and various other local notables made charming and witty dinner companions.

At night, on the way home on foot through one of the Oya villages, an old man came down from his house ahead of me on the path. He hurried along the path in my direction but as soon as he saw me he turned and rushed back and took up guard on the steps of his house until I had passed. Perhaps he suspected potential robbery and rape of the inmates.

A boy in songkok, sarong and baju, brought to my house a formally written invitation from the Tuan Bilal to attend a public reading of the Koran to be given by his daughter. This is a Muslim ceremony of importance as an indication that the young reader has completed reading the Koran in Arabic. The ceremonies began in the evening. The Tuan Bilal's house blazed with pressure lamps and a special verandah with a canopy had been built on to the front of the house for the occasion. This was on two levels, the higher one being for the more consequential guests. The order of precedence was maintained in the placing of the guests with a strictness which would have satisfied the matrons of the Faubourg Saint-Germain. The Koran was produced on a lectern and, starting at the head, was passed down the double row of guests each one reading a fairly lengthy passage. They knew very well that I was not a Muslim but, with great courtesy the holy book was placed before me to lead the readings. Fortunately I was familiar with the opening verses and was able to recite them. At the conclusion of the readings, hadzrah were chanted, almost interminably, by two groups of young men in alternation. They put their heart and soul into it and one group had no sooner finished, with a spirited series of drum beats, the lively concluding passage of its hadzrah, than the other group lustily commenced the andante movement of theirs. Meanwhile refreshments were being served in the most courtly fashion, on bended knees, on the upper verandah.

The following day the reading by the daughter took place. The preliminaries were much the same but the house was gaily decorated and on large tables outside were a host of skewered eggs hung with flags, miniature barong and posies of most artistic paper flowers, stuck on cigarette tins filled with saffron-coloured rice. These baubles were subsequently distributed to favoured guests.

I had been at a loss to know what present to make the

daughter in honour of this event and eventually selected the most expensive sarong which the bazaar had to offer from its limited and utilitarian collection. It was only when the procession arrived, wending its way from the house of her religious teacher, bearing her home in triumph, that I saw she was only a little girl—9 years old.

The Tooth of Buddha

Kandy in Sri Lanka is one of the fairest places in a country amongst the most beautiful on earth. It is also a place of considerable historical significance and of greater religious significance because of the presence there, in the great temple at the heart of Kandy, of a tooth of the Buddha. I arrived there as the representative of the Government of Sarawak to attend a United Nations seminar. The subject matter of the seminar was abuse of power by the executive of the state, a perennial weakness in the human element in systems of government. Power, as the eminent historian Lord Acton famously said, tends to corrupt and absolute power corrupts absolutely.

In his opening address, the then Prime Minister of Sri Lanka, Mr Bandaranaike, who was unfortunately assassinated a few weeks later, informed us that we were 'meeting amidst the dust of kings'. We got down to the more mundane matters of the conference but were astonished to hear towards the end of the conference that we were to be accorded the rare and signal honour of an exposition of the tooth. What was believed to be a tooth of the Buddha was kept in the Dalada Maligawa or Temple of the Tooth in Kandy. It was an object of the highest veneration by Buddhists.

The other delegates and I removed our shoes in the temple ante-chamber and, led by the ambassador of Burma—a devout Buddhist who reverently held an offering of frangipani blossoms in the open palms of his hands—were conducted up a narrow wooden staircase into a small wooden painted chamber barely large enough to accommodate us. The door to the chamber was locked behind us. The archpriests then opened two locked wooden doors at the end of the chamber to reveal an inner chamber filled with a padlocked iron cage. Inside the cage was a golden dagoba, a bell-shaped object with a spire, which can be seen all over Sri Lanka and other Buddhist countries in various sizes ranging to the colossal. This one was about the height of a man.

A bunch of keys was produced, the padlocks unlocked and the cage dismantled. The dagoba was lifted up to reveal another underneath and that in turn was lifted up to reveal another and so on until seven concentric dagobas had been removed. Each dagoba was draped with ropes of gold and precious gems, rich brocades and other offerings of the pious through the ages. These were piled in coruscating heaps on large trays as each covering was removed until the chamber began to resemble Aladdin's cave. This all took some time and the frangipani-scented air in the small chamber became stifling. Perspiration bathed those present but, in the interest of the moment, this was scarcely noticed. A gold gem-studded case reposing on a lotus flower of gold was the final container. When this was opened the tooth was revealed. It was placed with the greatest reverence on a special stand which, in turn, was placed on a golden cushion and covered by a glass bell. It was the colour of very old ivory. Its size was greater than one would have imagined a human tooth could be. Since one of the characteristics of the Buddha was his superhuman height this was to be expected.

The Buddhist delegates paid homage to the relic by kneeling and bowing low and the priests touched them lightly on the head with the cushion. The non-Buddhists were graciously invited to go forward, one by one, which we did and bowed with respect. The Hindu servant of one of the delegates, who had been admitted with Buddhist tolerance, at his earnest desire prostrated himself in front of the relic. There was no fuss but it was all very impressive.

After a few days spent visiting Anuradhapura and Polunnaruwa, remains of the ancient capitals of Ceylon, I happened to be back in Kandy on the night of Wesak, the great Buddhist festival commemorating the birth, enlightenment and passing of Gautama Buddha. As darkness fell one could see from the house where I was staying on a hill above the town, coloured illuminations all over the town and the surrounding hills. The Temple of the Tooth was ablaze with lights, which were reflected in the black mirror of the lake. The streets around the temple and the lake were crowded with people who had come in from all parts to see the perahera, the procession celebrating this special day. Little flare-lit stalls were busy supplying food, sweetmeats and drinks. From the temple came the insistent sound of drums and gongs. Within its precincts elephants were being girded and splendidly apparelled. Sundry persons in exotic attire were preparing themselves. Attendants bearing large, flaming, tarry torches wandered about, contributing lurid light and an element of risk.

At length, when all was ready, the procession began to form out of the inchoate mass. Men with thirty-foot whips came first, cracking them and clearing the way. Then followed the drummers, beating out alternately a slow rhythm and a fast exciting one. Brightly dressed Kandyan dancers with castanets followed, leaping and whirling, their faces solemn and fixed in concentration, apparently oblivious of the crowds and flaming torches. Then came a Kandyan nobleman, in a costume that betrayed mediaeval Portuguese influence, and his suite. The line of elephants appeared, preceded by agile and daring tumblers. The first elephant, gigantic and in gorgeous caparison, bore on his back an illuminated replica of the tooth. The illumination was supplied by a generator that was wheeled along at the very end of the procession. A long cable ran to the lead elephant and was attached along the way to numerous other elephants, with lighted bulbs dangling at frequent intervals. One presumes that electricity regulations, if there were any, were suspended for the occasion. The procession had scarcely begun when a cable parted and the illumination of the procession, save for the tarry torches, went out and were replaced by crackling blue and white flashes. One or two elephants began to look alarmed and were evidently contemplating sacrificing dignity for safety. But order was rapidly restored. An attendant appeared with insulating tape and the grand procession proceeded.

The mechanical arrangements may have been imperfect but the devotion of the people was unmistakable. As the procession passed by, the people joined their hands and bowed in homage, displaying the simple piety which had preserved the tooth for over two thousand years and created the great temples, frescoes and sculptures which adorn their country and stand as monuments to their civilization and the faith of man.

Sri Lanka is well known as a source of gemstones. I found a matching pair of coruscating blue zircons and brought them back to give to Yut, my maidservant, who had never had or even seen anything like them. She was, I could see, very delighted but with perfect Malay manners concealed her emotion and gravely thanked me. When I had occasion to visit Sarawak after my departure from it, I made a point of calling at Yut's house in the village. I was received by her father, a retired sergeant in the police, and her elder brother, a retired corporal. We had a polite conversation and I was waiting for Yut to appear. After a little time with no appearance of Yut, I asked after her and was told that she had passed away. The house seemed empty without her.

Prosecution and Deportation

Customs came to me with a report that a consignment of pepper had been underdeclared. There was an export duty on pepper, a great deal of which was being produced in Sarawak. A consignment of pepper in what were declared by the exporter to be hundredweight bags was in the customs warehouses on the river at Kuching. Some bags had been checked by the customs and found to be in excess of a hundredweight. The exporter was therefore evading duty by underdeclaring the weight. I asked for a list of the bags weighed by customs and a note of the weight of each. When this was supplied I paid a visit to the warehouse and had the bags produced and weighed in front of me while I checked the weights on the list. None, not one, of the weights on the list agreed with the weights in the customs list. I consulted the Director of Agriculture. He explained that peppercorns are highly sensitive to humidity and their weight will vary according to the degree of humidity at the time of weighing. The weight is therefore not constant and indeed can vary from day to day. That put paid to any idea the customs might have had of prosecuting the pepper exporters.

Some people think that the aim of the prosecutor is to obtain a conviction. This is not so. When a report of an alleged offence is referred to the prosecutor by the police or other authority, the prosecutor studies it in order to see whether the facts disclose a contravention of the law which merits prosecution. If they do, he will frame the appropriate charge giving brief details of the alleged contravention: the nature of the contravention, the date, time and place and the section of the law which is alleged to be contravened. The accused is brought before a court, the charge is read to him and he is asked whether or not he wishes to plead guilty. If he pleads not guilty a date is fixed for the trial and he is given or refused bail depending on the nature of the case.

However, before the prosecutor frames a charge he must be satisfied that there is *prima facie* evidence of an offence. *Prima facie* is a legal term and means that on the evidence available to the prosecutor it appears that an offence has been committed and that there is evidence which appears to justify a conviction. If there is insufficient *prima facie* evidence of an offence the prosecutor should not frame a charge and should notify the police or other authority accordingly. Of course the fact that there appears to be sufficient *prima facie* evidence does not necessarily mean that the accused person is guilty. When the hearing takes place it may be that the witnesses change their story or become confused or muddled or perhaps the report which the prosecutor has received is incomplete or misleading. Moreover there is the defence evidence to be considered by the court. This may throw an entirely different light on the facts, as it did in the rape case in Ayr.

Charging a person with an offence is a serious matter. It will cause anxiety to the accused person and his family and friends. It may be damaging to his reputation since some people may think there must be substance in the charge. It may damage his employment or business interests. It will also put him to the expense, if he can afford it, of engaging a lawyer to advise him and appear for him at the trial. These are not small matters and exercising the office of prosecutor is a heavy responsibility and requires the exercise of care both in the interest of the public and in the interest of the person accused. A prosecutor who is indifferent to this responsibility or worse, who is out to get a conviction, is unworthy of the office. It is emphatically not the duty of a prosecutor to seek a conviction or to press the court for a heavy sentence. His duty is to lay the facts calmly before the court, address the court on the relevant law and leave the rest to the court.

In another case, I received a report from the police in Kuching. This contained a complaint by a young man that he had paid a visit to a dentist in town for some professional attention. An anaesthetic was administered to him which reduced him to a semi-conscious state. While in this state he was indecently assaulted by the dentist. The only evidence available was the oral evidence of the complainant. In the statement taken by the police the dentist denied the accusation and said he did not administer an anaesthetic to the complainant. I informed the police that the dentist would not be charged. It is very easy to make this type of complaint, as it is of rape. If it goes to court it will be a case of one man's evidence against another. No court can find a charge proven beyond reasonable doubt, the standard of proof required in criminal cases, on this basis. To charge the dentist would result in highly damaging publicity to him and would not be justified unless there was some additional evidence supporting the complaint. In the Ayr case, there was the medical evidence of semen in the vagina of the complainant. This at least supported the allegation that there had been sexual intercourse and led to the charge of rape being made but again it came to one person's word against another and the evidence given by the accused person was more convincing than the evidence of the complainant. The prosecution was justified in that case but in the complaint against the dentist the sole evidence was the unsupported word of the complainant. This was not enough to justify proceedings.

In the late Fifties, communism was at its peak in China, there was a Communist rebellion in Malaya and Lee Kuan Yew, when he became Prime Minister in Singapore, was wrestling with the strong Communist movement there. The Communists were nearly all Chinese and we had a sizeable Chinese population in Sarawak. They possessed the admirable Chinese characteristic of being very keen on education for their children and there were Chinese schools in every town, but we knew there was Communist propaganda in some of these schools and there were teachers indoctrinating their pupils. Youngsters are idealistic and some of the Chinese youths were determined to emigrate to China which they regarded as the promised land. In fact since they were foreigners in China and from a part of the world the mainland Chinese refer to as the South Seas they were treated as inferiors. They spoke Chinese but their accent differed from the accents of mainland China and identified them as foreigners. Their identity papers also betrayed them. We tried to tell them this but they were not disposed to listen. We warned them that they would not be allowed to return: we did not want trained Communist agents in our community. It was to no avail for many who departed amidst tears from their families.

Special Branch is the department of the police that deals with intelligence and the surveillance of Communist activities. One day the locked despatch box in which secret papers for the Supreme Council were circulated arrived on my desk and I unlocked it with the special key held only by members of the Supreme Council. In it was a request by the Special Branch for a deportation order against a named Chinese. When I looked at the supporting paper I observed that it consisted of one short paragraph. This stated that the man was a teacher at a named Chinese school and that he was indoctrinating the youths at the school in communism. That was all. This was the first time that I had received such a request since I took over as Attorney General.

I was astonished that the police should apparently regard me as a rubber stamp to agree to anything they wanted without enquiry. I minuted on the paper that I was not prepared to authorize deportation, a very serious matter for the man concerned, without knowing what the evidence of indoctrination consisted of. The despatch box went back to the clerk to the Supreme Council who presumably notified the police accordingly. A few days later, a figure strode into my chambers unannounced, resplendent in uniform with lashings of gold braid and adorned with medal ribbons. This majestic figure was the Commissioner of Police, far senior to me in length of service. He stood, presumably for better effect, towering over my desk. He demanded to know why the request had not been granted. I pointed out that all I had been given was a bare, anonymous, allegation with no evidence whatever to support it. A deportation order can ruin a man's life, condemning him to exile from the land he was born and brought up in, where all his family and friends are and where his livelihood is. For all I knew, this allegation could have been made by someone who wanted to do him harm. What was required was details of the alleged indoctrination supported by written documents or witness statements and it was necessary to know where the information came from.

The Commissioner said: 'We do not disclose our sources of information.'

'What?' I said, 'not even to the Attorney General?'

'No,' he said.

'Well, then,' I said, 'I cannot approve the deportation order.'

The Commissioner was angry and said he would take the matter to the Governor. I replied that he was welcome to do whatever he considered proper. Whether he took the matter to the Governor or not, I do not know. The Governor would be very unlikely to interfere with a decision within the purview of the Attorney General. At any rate, I heard no more of the request for deportation. This suggests that the police had no evidence of weight to support the request and that the request had been made without proper consideration of the seriousness of what was being proposed and any proper consideration of what evidence would be required to justify it.

The Case of the Soekarno Lookalike

The tiny state of Brunei is totally surrounded by Sarawak. The sultans of ancient lineage, who for centuries exercised sovereignty over the larger part of the north east of Borneo, had ceded their territory piece by piece to the Brooke Rajahs. In the early years of the twentieth century the then sultan offered what remained of his territory to the British government in return for a very modest capital sum and an annuity. The offer was refused. It is ironic that the small territory they retained was discovered to be immensely rich in oil. It had become a protectorate of the United Kingdom and the senior officers of its government were seconded from Sarawak. It had few legal problems or major court hearings and these were dealt with by a judge from Sarawak and by the Sarawak Attorney General's chambers. There was no apparatus of democracy, the sultan was an absolute ruler although he was theoretically obliged by the protectorate to take the advice of a British Resident. The latter had to proceed with tact since the sultan, did not take kindly to advice on his policies and was not enthusiastic about the protectorate.

The capital's very first international hotel had opened its doors and was holding a launch party. Among those not invited was a gentleman named Chegu Salleh. Salleh had political aspirations, even though political parties were forbidden in Brunei, and he modelled himself on what he knew of Soekarno, the flamboyant President of Indonesia who was frequently in the media. Like Soekarno, Salleh wore a songkok and dark glasses and he went about town escorted by motorcycle outriders, young men dressed in black also sporting songkok.

The lack of an invitation was no deterrent to Salleh. The launch party was in full swing when the roar of motorcycles was heard outside and a few moments later Salleh swaggered in followed by his bodyguard. Shortly after that chairs were flying through the air and the party turned into a riot with guests fleeing the premises. The police arrived and the officer in charge, Pengiran Jaya, arrested Salleh and deposited him in a cell in the police station. The Chief of Police was informed and he went to the police station, was briefed on the affray, saw Salleh and offered to release him on bail. Salleh refused bail and threatened to sue Pengiran Jaya and the Chief of Police for wrongful arrest. Salleh was subsequently brought before a magistrate, convicted and was fined for the affray but, as he had threatened to do, he launched a High Court civil suit against the two police officers.

I travelled to Brunei to defend the police. On arrival I was approached by an emissary from the palace. Did I by any chance play chess. I am far from being a master but I had played chess since my schooldays. Subsequently I was invited to the palace, presented to His Highness, Sir Omar Ali Saifuddin, a gentle, retiring person, and he enquired whether I would care to play a game. We played and I won. His Highness's skill was even less than mine. He was quite surprised at his defeat. I can only presume that he had played with his subjects who either knew little about chess or thought it discourteous to defeat their ruler. However, His Highness asked me if I would like to have another game. We did and I took care to ensure victory for His Highness.

In the witness box at the trial of his suit, Salleh exhibited an aggressive personality. According to him, he entered the hotel peacefully and was arrested by the police for no reason at all. He was taken to the police station and lodged in a cell where he remained until he was brought before a magistrate who released him on bail. His cross-examination proved a little more illuminating.

Attorney General (A.G.): Did you receive any invitation to the opening of the hotel?

Salleh: No invitation was necessary. It was a hotel. Anyone can go there.

A.G.: When you arrived, were you accompanied by outriders on motorcycles?

Salleh: They are my people.

A.G.: And did they enter the hotel also?

Salleh: Some of them did.

A.G.: They were not invited either?

Salleh: No invitation was necessary.

A.G.: Very soon after your arrival fighting started and chairs and other objects were being used as weapons?

Salleh: I am not responsible for what happened.

A.G. Is it not the case that many of the guests were alarmed and were fleeing from you and your men?

Salleh: We were not involved in all that.

A.G.: Why do you think you were arrested?

Salleh: I do not know. The fighting had nothing to do with me.

A.G.: The police say that you were leading the fighting and that you and your men were causing the disturbance.

Salleh: That is not true

A.G.: The police also say that you were obviously under the influence of drink and that you were very aggressive.

Salleh: Not true.

A.G.: Is it a fact that you do drink?

(Alcohol is regarded by many Muslims as forbidden by the Koran and Brunei was an Islamic state. Salleh was a Brunei Malay and all Malays are Muslim. By Islamic law in Brunei, drinking would be an offence.)

Salleh: No it is not.

A.G. I regret that I must put it to you that you not only drink but that you habitually drink.

Salleh: It is not true.

(There was one bar and one bar only in Brunei, which was for expatriate oil workers and was not frequented by Malays. However I had been given a substantial number of bar chits which had been signed by Salleh. They bore numerous dates and were for hard liquor.)

A.G.: I must warn you that it is a criminal offence to give false evidence and that we have evidence that you habitually frequent a bar and drink there. I will give you the opportunity to retract your answer. I put it to you again that you do drink.

Salleh: No.

A.G.: I now produce and hand to you a bundle of bar chits for hard liquor which were signed by you.

Salleh: I don't agree.

A.G.: Are you saying that these are not your chits? We have the barman here who will give evidence.

Salleh: I refuse to answer the question.

A.G.: You adhere to your evidence that you do not drink?

Salleh: Yes.

The barman duly gave evidence and confirmed the chits were those of Salleh and that Salleh frequently came to the bar for a drink. The trial proceeded and the evidence demonstrated that the opening of the hotel was peaceful until Salleh and his gang arrived and that they caused the affray. The suit was dismissed.

I returned to Kuching and framed a charge of perjury against Salleh. Perjury is made a criminal offence by the Oaths and Affirmations Ordinance in Sarawak. This is a standard colonial Ordinance imposing the obligation on all witnesses in court proceedings of either taking the oath before giving evidence or affirming that what they are going to say is true. The formula administered to them by the Clerk of Court reminds them that it is a criminal offence to give false evidence.

On the plane back to Brunei for the trial I met the chief justice, who was going to hear the case. When we disembarked I discovered that I had not brought my passport. Going through immigration, the chief justice was immediately in front of me. When asked for his passport he said: 'I am the chief justice. I do not need a passport.' I was impressed and when I in turn was asked for my passport I said: 'I do not need a passport either. I am the Attorney General.' The immigration officer looked slightly stunned but the rule in this sort of situation is not to hesitate or appear uncertain but to walk steadily on as if there was no question hovering unanswered. It is true that both of us were gazetted in Brunei and clothed with official authority but we had no residential status and could properly be asked to produced our passports although it would have been unproductive to exclude us since Brunei needed both of us for the trial.

On arrival at my chambers in Brunei I reviewed the list of witnesses and their statements and checked the volumes of the *Laws of Brunei* for the Oaths and Affirmations Ordinance. There was no such Ordinance! This was a shock. I went through all the volumes of the *Laws of Brunei* yet again. It took me all night until dawn. I read every word of every Ordinance—perhaps there was a subsection tucked away somewhere which would help. No hope was too slim to pursue, no stone could be left unturned, hoping to discover somewhere a provision making perjury an offence. There was no such provision.

In court, the chief justice took his seat on the bench and I rose to address him. I informed him that the accused person was charged with perjury but I was unable to discover any provision of law in Brunei making this an offence. The chief justice bade me continue with the case and address him on the law at the end.

I called the witnesses. The evidence was incontrovertible. Salleh was an habitue of the bar and regularly consumed quantities of liquor there. He had in fact been there before going to the hotel on the night of the affray. So much for the facts. At the end of the evidence I again informed the court that there was no provision in the written laws of Brunei making it an offence to give false evidence. The law books available to me in Brunei were insufficient to allow me to ascertain whether the Common Law would fill the gap. The chief justice said: 'No one is going to come to my court and give false evidence with impunity.' He sentenced Salleh to six months jail.

There was, of course, an appeal, and I had to say to the Court of Appeal that I was unable to support the conviction. The Court of Appeal set aside the conviction and Salleh was released from jail but by that time he had served three months. His imprisonment was wrong in law but he was a thug, his lawsuit against the two senior police officers was a brazen piece of effrontery and the evidence he gave was a deliberate lie. Rough justice was done.

Departure from Sarawak

I was very happy in Sarawak. The colonial officers in the senior branch of the government service were not very many and I had friendly relations with almost every one of them in the various departments of government and also the judiciary and the police. I also had many friends amongst the various races. George had not approved of this but it did not prevent him recommending that I should be appointed to take his place when he had to leave.

The time came when I began to feel the need for a change of scene and fresh challenges. It was a painful decision to have to take. I loved the country and had got to know and love the people and to understand something of the culture and traditions of the many racial groups but I was in danger of getting into a groove with fixed ideas. Moreover I was given to understand that the colonial office would very likely soon be wanting to transfer me to another territory in accordance with their practice of moving officers around. I did not want to leave South East Asia but Malaya and Singapore were now independent and only British North Borneo, apart from Sarawak, remained as a colony and that was an unlikely posting, being a neighbour of Sarawak. Hong Kong was the likely posting since I was well-acquainted with Chinese culture and spoke some Mandarin. I had no desire to be posted to Hong Kong. I began to enquire about the possibility of practising at the Bar in Malaya and also Singapore. I received invitations from law firms in the capital city of Kuala Lumpur, from the university in Singapore, then known as the University of Malaya, and from Singapore law firms.

Some time before this there came to my attention proceedings in the High Court in Kuching regarding a trust. The Attorney General has a special responsibility to ensure that trusts are properly carried out and so the court sent copies of the papers to me. The trust fund consisted of very substantial assets. There were two competing groups of claimants to be the proper beneficiaries of the trust. Their opposing claims and the grounds for them were set out in the papers which they had filed. On studying these it did not seem to me that the claims of either side, as set out in the pleadings, were entirely sound. I decided to intervene.

The case went to a hearing in the High Court and the case for each group was presented by counsel. At the conclusion of their submissions I was invited to address the court as *amicus curiae*, that is to say as a neutral party to the dispute and with the object of assisting the court by presenting it with an impartial interpretation of the facts and the relevant law. The court then reserved judgement to consider the issues. Subsequently it issued judgement in favour of the group who, in my address, I had submitted were the proper beneficiaries.

A week or two later, I was informed by my clerk that some gentlemen had come to my chambers and wished to see me. They were ushered in. By their appearance they were eminently respectable Chinese gentlemen. I was not aware of having met them before. After the usual preliminary courtesies they informed me that they were the successful beneficiaries. They had come to present me with a token of their appreciation of my address to the court which, they considered, had resulted in their success. They then produced a package which they wished to give to me. I thanked them for their kind intention and explained that I was doing my duty as Attorney General and was not representing the interests of any party. Furthermore, by the general orders applicable to all colonial officers I was not allowed to receive presents. They were not so happy about this but after some attempts at persuasion went away.

Afterwards, following upon the various invitations which I had received, I flew to Kuala Lumpur for meetings with the law firms that had shown interest in me joining them and came to agreement with one of them. On return to Sarawak I submitted a letter to the Chief Secretary giving sufficient notice of resignation of the various offices which I held. Seven years had passed since I left Edinburgh and arrived in Sarawak. The decision to leave the Bar in Edinburgh and the ambience with which I was familiar had not been easy. It was a turning point in life. Now there was another turning point. I had become familiar and at home in Sarawak. I had no home elsewhere. Malaya had some features in common with Sarawak but there were major differences which I would have to get to recognize and adapt to. I had many friends in Sarawak and it was painful to part from them and go to live where I knew no one. It was a new start in life. I felt that I had served a purpose in Sarawak. However, as this sense of purpose was now waning I felt that it was time to go.

The time came to depart for Malaya. The *Rajah Brooke*, the vessel that sailed once a week to Singapore and back, was at the jetty in the Sarawak River in the middle of the town. The ship sailed on a Saturday after midday. It was the custom for friends of a departing officer to come aboard for a send-off cocktail party on deck before the ship sailed. Many colleagues in the government and friends of all races turned up to say goodbye. Amongst them I suddenly observed the Chinese gentlemen who had come to see me after the trust proceedings.

They approached me. 'We took note,' they said, 'that as Attorney General you were not allowed to receive presents.' 'That is right,' I said. 'Well,' they continued, 'you are not the Attorney General now and general orders no longer apply, so we believe that you can now accept this token of our thanks and we hope that you will not refuse it.' Indeed I could not. It would have been an affront to reject it and a considerable loss of face to these grateful and well-meaning gentlemen. I accepted it with heartfelt thanks at their kindness. When the ship sailed and I was alone in my cabin I opened the package and found a red velvet box which contained a pair of specially made gold cufflinks, each with a fine ruby on a crown mounting.